School Choices
True and False

School Choices

True and False

John Merrifield

The INDEPENDENT INSTITUTE

Oakland, California

The INDEPENDENT INSTITUTE   THE INDEPENDENT INSTITUTE is a non-profit, non-partisan, scholarly research and educational organization that sponsors comprehensive studies of the political economy of critical social, economic, legal, and environmental issues.

The politicization of decision-making in society has too often confined public debate to the narrow reconsideration of existing policies. Given the prevailing influence of partisan interests, little social innovation has occurred. In order to understand both the nature of and possible solutions to major public issues, The Independent Institute's program adheres to the highest standards of independent inquiry and is pursued regardless of prevailing political or social biases and conventions. The resulting studies are widely distributed as books and other publications, and are publicly debated through numerous conference and media programs.

Through this uncommon independence, depth, and clarity, The Independent Institute pushes at the frontiers of our knowledge, redefines the debate over public issues, and fosters new and effective directions for government reform.

THE INDEPENDENT INSTITUTE
100 Swan Way, Oakland, California 94621-1428, U.S.A.
Telephone: 510-632-1366 • Facsimile: 510-568-6040
E-mail: info@independent.org • Website: www.independent.org

Contents

1

Introduction

The persistent knowledge and critical thinking deficit among America's young people is deservedly one of the nation's top political issues. From presidential candidates to governors, every prominent policymaker calls K–12 reform a priority. But though reform fever is intense these days, widespread concern about the K–12 system is not new. Diane Ravitch, a top education official in the first Bush administration, said it was a major concern for most of the 1900s (Ravitch 2000, 23–27). Nuclear scientist Admiral Hyman Rickover's 1959 book blamed the K–12 system for the dangerous lack of scientific, engineering, and math talent in the United States, saying that "The system looks upon talented children primarily as a vexing administrative problem" (Rickover 1959). President Reagan's blue ribbon commission reached a similar but more strongly worded conclusion. Its 1983 report called the United States "a nation at risk," arguing that we have done something to ourselves that would be seen as an act of war if a foreign power were to blame (National Commission on Excellence in Education 1983). Those strong words produced an accelerated reform effort that continues to this day, but so far the reform frenzy has produced little more than micromanagement and frustration. The children discussed in *A Nation at Risk* have graduated from or dropped out of schools that even prominent Democrats—the strongest proponents of the current governance and funding process—call "a disaster" (Senator Gray Davis qtd. in Broder 1999; Kirkpatrick 1997; Senator Joseph Lieberman qtd. in Shokraii 1998).

This monograph defines and extends the argument for real competition in schooling, but its primary topics are the two reasons why the call for reform is so persistent and intense: (1) reform efforts have left existing governance and funding systems intact, and (2) choice advocates have forsaken and endangered the only truly effective reform catalyst—competition—mostly unwittingly, but often intentionally. Genuine competition is the only true reform catalyst. In the simplest terms, establishing competition means ending the government's policy of financial discrimination against families who prefer private schools or nontraditional public[1] schools and implementing flexible pricing, set by market forces, for education services. This monograph identifies and discusses the critical elements of a competitive education industry, describing the foreseeable outcomes of competition and the transition to it.

Current parental choice programs and nearly all the prominent choice proposals are too small and contain too many restrictions to harness market forces effectively, yet much of the rhetoric asserts the presence of competition. The resulting combination of high expectations and low potential for improvement might be politically devastating. Lackluster "results" from alleged experiments might broadly tarnish parental choice programs. Deeming current programs successful may only prompt the duplication of restriction-laden, escape-hatch versions of parental choice.

A brief review of the failures of K–12 education and the reasons for those failures is a useful first step before turning to the failures of the K–12 reform debate and what must be done to create true improvement.

2

Where We Stand: The Achievement Deficit

Because "stories of academic mediocrity have become so common that they have lost power to shock" (Coats 1997, 10), I am leaving the task to other sources (Murphy 1996, 139–48; Vedder 2000, 5–9). Instead, I mention some of the more subtle symptoms of failure, discussing a few of them in more detail later on.

The incredible growth in home schooling may be the most compelling symptom of our system's failure (Brandly 1997; "Explosion in Home Schooling" 1996). Many parents give up careers to do the work of teams of education specialists whom they have already paid and typically outperform them by a wide margin. Home-schooled children are highly sought after college recruits. Yet educating children is not easy, and the advantages of specialization apply to schooling as to any other trade or profession. If it were not for the profound failure of public schools, it would be no more likely that home schooling would produce superior results than, say, home television repair.

Another symptom of failure is parental apathy. Despite widespread concerns about K–12 performance, the high cost of exiting the public schools (which supposedly should lead to more "voice"),[2] and the pressure "to get involved in public schools" (Lowe and Miner 1996), the vast majority of parents make little effort to influence the practices of their own schools (Dixon 1992; Pierce 1993). Multiple levels of political control make parents feel powerless and give educators little leeway in addressing their concerns. In addition, educators have little incentive to heed parents' concerns.

Educators' paychecks depend on pleasing public officials, not on serving children.

State takeovers are another symbol of failure and frustration. Since 1988 the states have taken over twenty local school systems, including schools in Boston, Baltimore, Chicago, Cleveland, Hartford, Newark, Philadelphia, and Washington, D.C. (School Reform News 1999). State takeovers unfortunately elicit only additional frustration and fail to yield significant improvement. Even in those schools that have had a positive takeover experience, significant improvement has meant approaching merely the national norms of "a nation at risk."

Other cities—among them Milwaukee, the site of the nation's most famous school choice program—are on the brink of a takeover. The Milwaukee Public School (MPS) situation reflects both of the problems cited earlier: its reform efforts left existing governance and funding systems intact, and the additional rivalry created by Milwaukee's small low-income voucher program falls far short of the truly competitive conditions necessary to prompt real reform.

The system's persistent failings are not an accident. The problems begin with the baneful effects of monopoly. The activists and public officials who refuse to consider any fundamental changes in funding and governance denounce the monopoly label. They correctly fear it. Americans rightly associate monopoly with consumer helplessness, producer sloth and indifference, and high prices. Defenders of the status quo point to the system's highly fragmented nature, multiple layers of oversight, and nearly fifteen thousand school districts (Lowe and Miner 1996) as evidence that it is not a monopoly. Still, the monopoly label is appropriate. The number of districts in a metropolitan area matters only a little bit. The number nationwide is nearly irrelevant. Monopoly is not just a matter of numbers (whether one or many), but rather of openness to new producers and significant changes in market share.

The public-school monopoly stems from the fact that the neighborhood public school usually has a huge price advantage over any potential competitors, including other public schools. Using a public school outside a family's attendance area requires significant transportation spending, the risk of incurring criminal sanctions with a false address, or a change of residence and potentially higher home prices. An average private school costs more than $3,000 per child in addition to the school taxes that must be paid, which is why there aren't many private schools. Entrepreneurs are theoretically free to enter the market for K–12 services, but it is very difficult to beat a zero-tuition competitor that has more resources.

As you would expect from a monopoly, public schools are inefficient and charge taxpayers a high and ever-rising sum. The public-school system's administrative overhead is one example of its inefficiency. According to an international comparison by the Organization for Economic Cooperation and Development (OECD 1995), the United States is the only country with fewer teachers than nonteaching staff—a three to four ratio. The average teacher to nonteaching staff ratio is five to two.

Failure to achieve continuous improvement is another symptom of monopoly. The school system does not pursue research and development systematically or spread effective practices (Miller 1999). Technological backwardness is the norm. Public schools buy many computers and connect them to the Internet, but technology is usually something to teach rather than a teaching tool. There is no discernible propensity to systematically root out unproductive practices and practitioners (Lieberman 1993). Dale Ballou and Michael Podgursky (1997) reported that public schools give little weight to the quality of teachers' credentials and rarely terminate unproductive teachers.

Reform Resistant

Monopolies may change, but they rarely reform. The public schools have changed, probably too much as educators flit from one fad to the next, but very little of that change has been productive.

Wayne Jennings coined a good label for this process: so far the reform frenzy amounts to a "more of the same harder (MOTS-H)" (1998, 1). An anonymous "Horse Story" makes the same point: "If the horse you're riding dies, get off, . . . in the education business we don't always follow that advice."[3] Both MOTS-H and the "Horse Story" refer to a propensity to recycle acts of proven futility that can make things worse directly or do so indirectly by adding to a constant parade of marginal change that drives educators crazy. With multiple levels of political oversight, forced change can produce burnout, frustrating contradictions, and debilitating and humiliating micromanagement.

Like many other places, Milwaukee describes its reform efforts as "decades of frustration" (White 1999, 34). Consider just the past fourteen years. Probably because of the media attention generated by the 1983 *A Nation at Risk* report (see Peterkin 1996), supposedly major reforms occurred in 1987. Persistent disappointment and media attention generated by Milwaukee's unique parental choice program prompted additional reform efforts during the 1990s, and yet Milwaukee still just barely averted a June 2000 state takeover. There are no reasons to expect a different outcome from current or future efforts to wring better outcomes from the current system. Until we implement real reform, the incentives will be the same or weaker.

The current reform-resistant system elicits statements from leading scholars and civil rights leaders that you usually hear only from knee-jerk, antigovernment cynics. The system is much worse than inefficient. It unwittingly but effectively undermines learning. Harvard's Caroline Hoxby concluded a study this way: "The striking thing is the opposite directions of the spending and achievement results: less spending, more student achievement" (qtd. in Barro 1997). Hoxby's conclusion is consistent with National Urban League President Hugh Price's belief "that politicians and school administrators are going about the business of improving things exactly backwards" (Price 1999, 76). Rexford Brown assailed a widespread, underachievement-assuring definition of success: "Success in urban school districts is often defined as the avoidance of large-scale violence. . . . managers define success as the absence of an angry mob of customers sacking the store and assaulting the employees" (1993, 137). Teachers frequently define success within those limitations: "We're doing a good job. You can go to any other district and see they are having the same type of problems" (Walsh 1999b, 46-51). It is precisely because the system's consistent problems and unacceptable output are the net result of mostly dedicated, conscientious teachers that we so desperately need to transform the system.

In today's system, school leaders don't celebrate unexpected success stories, study them, and then seek to imitate them. Instead, they seem to fear surprises. As Nobel Laureate John Hicks once wrote, "The best of all monopoly profits is a quiet life" (Hicks 1935). In a political environment, exceptional achievements raise questions and expectations that can force change and generate more work for the same paycheck. As a result, recognition can mean endangerment rather than duplication. Fear of higher expectations also encourages uniformity.[4] In one especially telling example, an incoming district superintendent cut an innovative school with an undisputed record of success because "the school was too autonomous. . . . [I]ts efforts to maintain a racial balance and its insistence on being different made it elitist, too much like a private school" (Meier 1991, 338).

The system resists energetic reformers and high standards. Former superintendents Anthony Trujillo (Ysleta District of El Paso, Texas) and Diana Lam (San Antonio District, Texas) implemented major reforms, and test scores rose (Trujillo 1999). Not long after gaining national attention, including considerable acclaim, Trujillo's and Lam's contracts abruptly were terminated at considerable cost to taxpayers. In addition, the fact that "the education standards movement is gaining momentum" (Price 1999, 54-55, 76) means that you need semipermanent political organizations to lobby for high standards and that you face considerable opposition.

Failure to Specialize Brought About by Political Control

Specialization is a cornerstone of productivity. This idea rests on the irrefutable fact that consumers have diverse preferences and that producers have unique skills, talents, and interests. But the current system officially attacks or denies child and educator diversity, thus precluding any meaningful degree of specialization.[5] The use of attendance zones means that every school must attempt to address diverse interests, skills, and learning styles. Schools with attendance areas can't specialize. Policies that mandate nonselective admissions policies undermine specialization functionally and politically. For example, a school can't specialize in gifted and talented children if they can't turn away parents suffering delusions of grandeur (Johnny isn't always as bright as mom and dad imagine him to be). The huge mismatches that would result from assigning children to specialized schools would also be politically infeasible.

There is another major political problem. The collective hostility to specialization is as deeply ingrained as the individual consumer's preference for it. The need for a specialized school to be selective is seen as a guarantee of taboo forms of discrimination. The political process greatly diminishes public-school effectiveness whenever it translates that collective hostility into an official antidiscrimination policy. This inability to be selective is widespread because anything with a potential connection to segregation is a political third rail.

Choice opponents take every opportunity to exploit and reinforce this collective hostility. They depict selectivity in any form as actual or imminent discrimination by a public heavily populated with racists whose top priority is to flee schools with significant minority populations. They insist on crippling educators with nonselective admissions policies or with random admissions when demand exceeds capacity.

The inability of public schools to specialize is in part responsible for the belief that choice will worsen the segregation we already have. Because nearby schools usually have similar policies, location and student body composition can easily become key choice criteria by default. With the differences in subject matter, size, and methodology that specialization would create, there are at least two reasons why parental choice probably will produce increasingly diverse student bodies:[6] (1) subject and pedagogy preferences usually will dominate racial/ethnic homogeneity preferences, and (2) improvement through competition will reduce the inverse correlation between wealth and minority membership. Parental choice that fosters competition will produce less-diverse student bodies only if homogeneity preferences are widespread and dominate other school differences, if academic preferences are highly correlated with group membership, or if school operators can ignore the antidiscrimination laws easily. Each is extremely unlikely.

The nearly universal attendance-area policy, fear of discrimination claims, and overreaction to the "common school" mythology have led to the policy of teaching nearly every child the same things in approximately the same way. This approach is even spelled out in some state constitutions and major court rulings. Schools have to attempt to make themselves into one-size-fits-all institutions. Standardized testing reinforces that pressure because its use in ranking schools and allocating resources presumes that quality is one-dimensional. In contrast, we know that particular people and businesses are good at some things but not at others. Even if schools defy the barriers and disincentives and pursue the one-size-fits-all imperative as well as possible, the result still won't be very good.

Against common sense and centuries of experience, the current system implicitly assumes that the political process can create coherent education policies in the face of historically intractable controversies over curriculum content, expectations, and the scope of appropriate school services. In addition, the governance of the current system assumes that the politically palatable outcome is best for virtually everyone. Sheldon Richman summarizes the history accurately: "All of this [curriculum content legislation] is premised on the idea that a good school curriculum is uncontroversial. That's nonsense. An uncontroversial curriculum is as bogus as a value-free education" (2001).

Political Control of the Curriculum

Textbook content, curriculum, and testing are increasingly politically sensitive (Sykes 1995, chap. 10). Allegations that test questions and entire tests are biased against certain groups are common. The increasing importance of political correctness has made textbooks dumber, duller, and more misleading. History texts omit and distort major events and figures to appease vocal special interests. Literature suffers "reconstruction" and even math texts are controversial (Holland 2000). Publishers are "whipsawed by pressure groups ranging from evangelical Christians to feminists, homosexuals, peace activists, environmentalists, and secular humanists to accommodate their agendas and priorities. Pandering to interest groups takes precedence over literary and even factual considerations" (Sykes 1995, 132). The political responses to controversy (deletion, dilution, distortion) are extremely debilitating.

Lack of Incentives

The policies that underlie the current system implicitly assume that incentives—good and bad—don't matter. The connection between client satisfaction and resources for producers is weak at best and often appears backward. Failure rather than success often earns additional resources. It's a mistake to think that additional funds for especially bad schools will not pepetuate (and perhaps even encourage) failure.

Government's habit of making the appearance of fairness an imperative makes merit pay rare and adds to the inherent problems of measuring and rewarding merit in the public sector. Merit policies for government employees such as teachers easily can create as many perverse incentives as desired ones. In government, gauging performance is difficult, and the link between merit and the employer's ability to reward it is weak at best. Better schooling can increase public-school funding only gradually by driving up property values, and the benefits don't necessarily find their way to the best schools. They are spread across the entire district. In many states, funding equalization lawsuits and a reduced reliance on property taxes have weakened or cut the already tenuous link between merit and revenue.

Public-sector merit pay is virtually a zero-sum game, and administrative measurement inevitably narrows educators' attention to the specific factors to be measured, including factors such as test scores or teachers' performance during periodic classroom observations by their principal. Still important but not specifically measured items will suffer neglect. For example, suppose merit is based on standardized math and reading test scores. Spending additional time on math and reading, test-taking strategies and practices, and skills specific to the particular test diminishes instruction in other areas. Furthermore, government agencies' merit-raise budgets are typically fixed, so a merit raise for one person comes at the expense of another, which can discourage cooperation and limit the positive incentive effects to the few people who exhaust the merit-raise budget.

Contrast this situation with merit pay in the private sector, where it is not a zero-sum game. Because there is no externally fixed budget, every employee can earn a raise of any size. And at least for the business as a whole, merit is easily observed in the bottom line. Because businesses typically face more competitive labor markets than school districts do, they are also much more likely to recognize meritorious behavior with a raise.

3

Problems of the Reform Debate

Ends-Means Confusion

Our system is so old that most people equate schooling with tax-funded, government-run schools. The strong tendency to confuse the means (taxes for public schools) with the goal (educating children) helps the governance and funding process resist change. "Criticism of [the means] is portrayed as an attack on the end itself" (Quade 1996). The system is so deeply entrenched that elimination of the penalty for using private schools is seen as public support for another school system. Even conservatives such as Representative Marge Roukema (R-N.J.) see education funding in terms of systems, not children: "No matter how proposals of relief for private school costs are designed, the ultimate effect is to burden the taxpaying public with support of two school systems" (qtd. in Voliva 1999). And many choice advocates silently accept major, crippling elements of the status quo. For example, choice advocates usually assume the permanence of school cartels called districts and their immense bureaucracies.[7]

Pervasive, Disorienting Fallacies

One of the most prominent fallacies regarding reform is the idea that only the worst schools are bad. For example, because suburban schools are usually much better than inner-city schools, many people believe that suburban schools are at least okay. But severely underprepared college freshman, declining test scores, students' widespread inability to answer easy questions[8] or to demonstrate basic literacy (Finn 1995), and their poor analytical skills say otherwise. Colleges spend growing millions on remediation, and businesses teach basic skills to entry-level workers. A recent international comparison of students' math and science skills is the latest evidence that even our best students are not competitive ("Third International Mathematics" 1998, 1). And the huge deficiencies of suburban public schools are commonplace and well documented.[9] "Millions of middle class children [are] emerging half-ignorant from suburban schools," says former assistant secretary of education Chester Finn (Finn 1995). "Even the best students did miserably. At the top scoring schools, the average was well below grade level" (Kantrowitz and Wingert 1991). Many of the best schools are still inadequate.

The problem is a low-performing system, not isolated low-performing schools. Most private schools are also inadequate because of the tax-dollar monopoly of public schools and because the system discourages private spending on K–12. Students at private schools typically score somewhat higher on achievement tests than those at public schools and they are much more likely to finish high school and attend college—even after rigorously controlling for student attributes (e.g. Evans and Schwab 1995)—but the private sector, as it exists today, is not a shining model. Private schools are much more cost-effective, but the vast majority must operate on the cheap to compete with "free" public schools.[10] We need reform because the current system lavishes resources on the inefficient, politically controlled public sector but starves the more efficient, potentially more effective private sector.

Despite this similarity, it is widely assumed that the system takes good care of the affluent.[11] They supposedly have school choice. They can live in the suburbs or use private schools. But the failure to discern the difference between better and good usually leaves them with only a false sense of security. Even the affluent often end up in inadequate schools. And the apparent access to alternatives reduces the political pressure for systemic reform. Because quality-conscious choice applicants are often more prone to political activity (Hirschman 1970), the availability of a seemingly reasonable substitute can weaken the pressure to produce meaningful reform.

The fallacy that top schools are good schools shunts reform efforts into tinkering that does not effect systemic transformation. For example, the Texas voucher proposals and Florida's new program (Sandham 1999)[12] address students in "low-performing" schools—officially less than 10 percent of schools even though more than 40 percent of the children lack basic skills. In the Florida program, children can't use vouchers until they are severely undereducated for two to four years,[13] and then they are told to try to do better in the private sector with about half the money per student available to a public school. The caps on participation and private spending preempt competition and reform.[14]

Many analysts claim that socioeconomic factors, not school conditions, explain the achievement deficit. Indeed, Frederick Hess found that "the most significant determinants of educational success are the student's socioeconomic background and familial context" (1998, 13). So school differences supposedly don't explain academic deficiencies. Hess and some of his sources conclude that "Social measures that target the home and neighborhood environments of disadvantaged children might prove more effective than educational remedies"(1998, 13). But the analysts do not recognize the fact that although a statistical analysis will explain differences from the average, it will not explain why the average is high or low. The proper interpretation of statistically insignificant school characteristics is that the impact of schools on intellectual growth is consistent—that is, consistently bad because academic outcomes are appalling where socioeconomic conditions are the worst and only dismal where socioeconomic conditions are good.

An overly static outlook is frequently part of the ends-means confusion. Even prominent choice advocates take many parts of the status quo for granted. The symptoms are plentiful. Though the essential outcome of choice is a transformation of available options, including private schools, even prominent choice advocates assume that key parts of the current public system will persist. They most often mistakenly assume (1) that the current menu contains all the possible choices; (2) that including private schools in a choice program doesn't make sense unless existing private schools significantly outperform current public schools; (3) that the private sector will remain largely nonprofit and church run, with a few expensive, very select schools; (4) that the excess capacity of existing private schools defines the upper limit on participation in parental choice programs; and (5) that an expansion of the private sector will force some teachers to accept lower salaries.

The February 1998 issue of the *Mobilization for Equity* newsletter contains an especially glaring example of these fallacies and of the debilitating conclusions they foster. It claims that private schools don't have "enough [empty] seats. The majority of students will be forced to remain in the public system *regardless of how voucher programs are implemented*" (1998, 1, 3, emphasis added). That's dangerous nonsense! The private sector's minimal excess capacity only ensures that public schools will have time to improve. And if the public schools fail to make themselves choiceworthy, the private sector will slowly achieve dominance. A truly competitive system contains no upper limit on the size of the private sector.

The static outlook symptoms are typically more subtle. Based on the excess capacity of Catholic schools, Peter Cookson claims that "you could get some competition quicker if you included private schools in a choice plan, but it wouldn't be much more competition" (1996, 252). Stan Karp argues that "this [the free market] meant [turning the education system over to] the local Roman Catholic Archdiocese" (qtd. in Lowe and Miner 1996, 32), which had approximately one thousand vacancies. Linda Darling-Hammond says that "Vouchers are a smokescreen," a distraction from critical equity issues because there are only a "limited number of slots worth choosing" (qtd. in Lowe and Miner 1996, 12). Robert Lowe and Barbara Miner believe a voucher system would force parents "to compete for a few select schools" (1996, 14–15).

The assumption of minimal systemic change—based on the belief that school taxes exist to support public schools rather than children—underlies the common assumption that vouchers or tax credits would be very small. In such a world, children would be able to leave the government system but would take only few, if any, public funds with them. Vouchers or tax credits supposedly then would be useless to most families but a windfall for the wealthy. The idea that "Poor parents cannot afford to pay the difference between a voucher and a private school's full tuition" (Fondy 1998) stems from the implicit assumptions that vouchers would be small and that there would be few low-cost private schools. However, even with such an anticompetitive voucher policy, the claim is in part false. The determination of some low-income families and the low tuition at some private schools have combined to generate considerable demand for vouchers available only to low-income families (Goldwater Institute 1994).[15]

With an appropriate, strictly child-based funding policy (that is, existing public K–12 dollars fund children at the same level whether they enroll in a public or private school), claims that only the rich would benefit are utterly false. In a truly competitive system, public money alone would give every family access to all but the most elite prep schools, and a truly competition-oriented policy would further expand access to schools by allowing families to supplement their share of public funds with their own money. Most private schools would have much more money per student than they do under the current system. That and the competitive pressures would improve private schools greatly and possibly cause public schools to behave competitively. Because low-income families often have children in below-average public schools, they have the most to gain from the improvement and greater availability of private schools, not to mention from the possible improvements in the public schools.

Reform versus Limited Escape

There is a mismatch between existing reform rhetoric and policy proposals that recycle acts of proven futility or just move a few children within the system. Tinkering with the system can help some children, but they're not rescued. Small improvements to a few schools and limited escapes from terrible schools leave many behind and leave the system intact.

Debilitating fallacies, inadequate understanding of market systems, and overreaction to political defeats have shifted the parental choice debate to escape-valve policies that cannot produce reform. Unless choice advocates quickly and assertively shift their primary focus back to policies capable of establishing real competition, one of two likely effects seems certain: (1) parental choice will be seen only as a marginal change aimed at helping disadvantaged children, or (2) if the resource-starved private schools that enroll most of the public-school escapees don't significantly outperform the public schools, parental choice will be seen as an ineffective tool. But a comparison of resource-poor private schools and politically crippled public schools is misleading and meaningless. The whole system is broken, and competition would transform both.

4

Problems with Current Voucher and Choice Reforms

Market forces have an awesome track record, even in K–12 education (Coulson 1999). Still, there is caution and lots of talk about experiments. But existing "experiments" don't test market forces; they ration choice and only slightly diminish discrimination against private-school users. Some even create de facto price controls.

Important versus Trivial Experiments

In "a nation at risk," only policies capable of transforming the system truly deserve the "experiment" label. The current parental choice programs—I discuss specific programs shortly—don't qualify. Mind you, they help thousands of children, and the programs' creators deserve our respect and admiration. I'm glad they exist as escape hatches. But because none of the current programs can significantly change the systems in which they exist or tell us how competition would transform a school system, they are not important experiments.

Consider a restaurant analogy. If a bunch of people are stuck in a reform-resistant restaurant, you can at least direct them toward better items on the menu. That's what the Florida, Milwaukee, and Cleveland programs do and what most privately funded programs do.[16] But the real problem is the unacceptable menu, and existing parental choice programs leave the menu largely intact and give just a few families access to better items. An experiment worthy of the name would test ways to prompt drastic menu changes.

We know from extensive experience behind the Iron Curtain that "freedom" to shop at the best government stores is not a reform catalyst. Public-school choice, including charter schools, will not transform our school system any more than the freedom to choose a state-owned store transformed the Soviet Union.

The claim that competition exists in Milwaukee and Cleveland or through public-school choice programs deceives many people. Alongside the glowing praise from choice advocates and the media hype surrounding the parental choice debate, the modest effects of such limited programs may cause the public to conclude that "competition" is an ineffective reform catalyst.

Real competition *is* a reform catalyst, so a well-designed demonstration project might convince people who do not understand the history or economics of a free market in education.[17] In this demonstration, we would have to establish the critical elements of competitive markets, including universal access and nondiscrimination by the government (described in detail later), in at least one well-populated region.[18] Any of the certifiably reform-resistant urban areas, with school systems so bad that no imaginable transformation can make things worse, would be perfect sites for a demonstration of the "Competition: Tried and True" axiom. Similar regions maintaining the status quo would serve as benchmarks.

Typical Debilitating Restrictions of the Alleged Market Experiments

The most common and significant restriction in market experiments is the participation level. In Milwaukee, the largest publicly funded voucher program caps participation at 15 percent. Only low-income parents can receive public funds for tuition. In Florida, participation by children in officially certified, chronically low-performing schools seems certain to stay far below 15 percent.

Schools have to achieve only a grade of "D" in three out of four years to deny even the cheapest exit option to their victims. The state grades itself, so certified chronic failure is sure to be rare. The Cleveland program remains tiny even though the litigation that culminated in the recent Supreme Court ruling highlighted the dismal condition of Cleveland's public schools. The private Edgewood voucher program in San Antonio, Texas, offers virtually every resident of a small part of the metropolitan area enough money to attend nearly every existing private school, but the other privately funded programs only partially support a tiny fraction of the children in the places where such programs exist.

Another significant restriction is the continued discrimination against parents who prefer private schools. Public-school choice programs do not diminish that discrimination at all, and existing voucher and tax credit programs reduce it only slightly. *At best*, private-school users typically receive a little more than half as much public money per child as public-school users. Discrimination against private-school users puts private schools under considerable financial duress. Only a relative few are able to perform the near miracle of getting people to pay a second time for a private-sector substitute produced much more cheaply than prepaid public schooling available at no additional charge.

The Florida and Milwaukee programs preclude the use of the private funds that could diminish the effect of financial discrimination. In both places and in many proposals, private schools cannot cash vouchers unless they accept them as full payment. They must compete for students and teachers with less money per student. The larger the voucher program, the more such bans on private money add-ons resemble de facto price controls. For example, suppose that some families are eligible for $3,000 vouchers and that add-ons are banned. Only ineligible families will purchase services that cost slightly more than $3,000. For eligible families, $3,001 worth of schooling will cost them $3,001 more than $3,000 worth of schooling. They won't pay thousands more for a few dollars worth of extra services. A universal program that bans add-ons would eliminate services that cost slightly more than the voucher amount. The private sector would contain only cheap private schools that charge the voucher amount and elite schools that charge much more than the voucher amount. Because the seriousness of add-on bans is so poorly understood, I give this issue additional attention later.

Trivial, Irrelevant, and Misleading Evaluation Criteria

The current alleged experiments weren't set up to generate data, and they lack a clearly stated hypothesis. There is no link between the critical issue of system transformation and the implied hypothesis evident in statements such as, "The success or failure of school choice hinges on hard statistical data: Are choice students' test scores higher than those of their public school peers?" (McGroarty 1996). But test score comparisons based on a limited parental choice program can only indicate whether choice applicants are good judges of narrowly defined school differences. Parents will compete for vouchers and private-school space only when they believe that these things will secure better schooling. Test score data may not reflect the factors that prompted parents to apply for a voucher (and test scores become a major political issue once hype attaches unwarranted significance to so-called experiments), but even if test score data reflect the factors that parents value the most, the alleged "experiment" will produce no significant insight. I strongly suspect that most thoughtful people already believe that active parents can tell which school will achieve the best results for their children. Research to see if voucher applicants can tell which school is best for their child is trivial. That proposition is intuitive and believable without empirical evidence.

Because test score data may not reflect the reasons parents preferred a private school and analytical errors can easily misrepresent effects, even studies of "hopelessly obvious"[19] issues can easily create misleading impressions. The image of parental choice as a reform catalyst can be badly tarnished by a good analysis of bad or irrelevant data, or by a bad analysis of good data. For example, recently published results from one parental choice program show gains only for African American "escapees" (Clowes 2000b, 1, 6). Even though the four programs (New York, Washington, Dayton, and Charlotte) that produced the results foster only miniscule movement within the system, the media hype may leave many people with the false impression that parental choice is a quite limited, weak tool. Whatever the reason for a weak showing by the choosers, the headlines will associate "choice" with "ineffective." Many people will not read the fine print or rebuttals, and even if they do, the rebuttals, with the resulting aura of controversy, only create confusion, a major impediment to change. Indeed, at least six publications already claim that the data generated by the alleged experiments demonstrate that parental choice is an unproductive reform, (Economic Policy Institute 1993; Carnegie Foundation 1992; TSTA/NEA 1994; Elmore, Orfield, and Fuller 1995; Smith and Meier 1995; Drury 2000) and the rebuttals have produced only confusion and hype that legitimize caution about change. According to Terry Moe's (2001) survey, perceived risk was the major reason for public resistance to voucher proposals.

In the typical voucher program discussion, the program is seen as effective only if voucher recipients outperform the unsuccessful voucher applicant control group. Because an experiment is invalid if the "treatment" affects the control group, designating the unsuccessful voucher applicants as the control group amounts to an assumption that the voucher program will not prompt changes in public schools. Furthermore, the published evaluations ignore the negative impact that restricted choice programs could potentially have on current private-school users. Add-on restrictions, for example, will tend to reduce the tuition and therefore spending per-student and may thus encourage private schools to increase class sizes or in other ways lower quality. In other words, the typical evaluation methods (Greene, Peterson, and Du 1997) implicitly assume away public- and private-sector change!

If the public schools react positively to rivalry for students and cause the unsuccessful voucher applicants to improve as much as the voucher users, the program is an effective reform catalyst. However, because such an effect would minimize the differences between the voucher users and the unsuccessful applicants, present evaluation methods would make the program seem ineffective! Meanwhile, escape-valve programs that merely provide a better option for some students would look especially effective.

Comparisons between the relatively few voucher users and unsuccessful applicants also create the illusion that parental choice can produce only a slightly larger version of the current private sector. The small, restriction-laden voucher and tax credit plans that get nearly all the attention would do that, but we should not dismiss other possibilities or give the public the impression that other options don't exist. We need a much higher standard than the current private sector. Parental choice—indeed any policy proposal worthy of the title "reform"—must improve both public and private schools significantly.

Comparisons between typically resource-starved private schools and strait-jacketed, undermotivated public schools are not useful. Indeed, they endanger reform. Most readers of the initial Greene, Peterson, and Du (1997) Milwaukee study probably wondered why anyone would prefer the three private schools that enrolled more than 80 percent of the initial voucher recipients. That the forsaken public schools must have been even worse will not engender excitement about the apparent options created by "school choice." Such comparisons can only lower expectations for parental choice programs and harden teacher opposition.[20]

5

Examples and Additional Context from Programs and Proposals

Milwaukee

The eleven-year-old Milwaukee program began as a tiny escape hatch for poor children stuck in reform-resistant schools. One percent of Milwaukee Public Schools' (MPS)'s low-income users used tax dollars at a secular private school willing to admit them for approximately half the public-school budget per student. Voucher users could not exceed half of a private school's enrollment, and the schools had to accept the voucher as full payment. That severely limited the school choices; at first, 80 percent of the voucher users attended just three troubled private schools. Despite that limitation and MPS efforts to discourage voucher use, the demand still greatly exceeded voucher availability.

Since then, the escape hatch has widened. The cap is up to 15 percent of the MPS population; private schools no longer face a non-voucher minimum enrollment; and church-run schools can participate. However, virtually every study of the Milwaukee program relies on data from the smaller, original program. And key competition-killing restrictions remain, including the still-severe participation cap, the de facto price controls (schools must accept vouchers as full payment), and a big gap between the voucher value and the MPS funding per student. The latter two restrictions probably explain why private-school capacity rather than the number of vouchers now limits voucher use.[21]

Though there were significant differences in the approaches and conclusions of the various evaluators (Davis 1996), they all used the unsuccessful voucher applicants as the benchmark to determine whether the voucher users were better off. Not only did they make no effort to look for MPS responses to the voucher program, but they also implicitly assumed there would be none. They also ignored the possible effects of changed budgets and changes in class size and composition on the nonvoucher private-school users.

Though the true bottom-line issue under investigation is trivial—Can active parents pick the school option that is best for their children?—the evaluation criteria stated in the enabling legislation were right for a tiny escape hatch. Polly Williams, the author of the legislation, and her supporters weren't trying to reform the MPS.

Even though the voucher program created no concrete incentives to improve education (other than more media attention), there are still periodic claims that it caused improvements in MPS. In an unpublished conference paper, Caroline Hoxby says that the public schools with the most voucher-eligible students showed the largest (though still tiny) academic gains (or smallest losses) per dollar spent. Prior to Hoxby's paper, the only alleged evidence that the voucher program was responsible for improvements was school board members' willingness to sign a voucher fund-raising letter (Rees 1999b) and minor policy changes such as promises to spend more taxpayer money on remedial summer instruction (Williams 1998).

Florida, Texas, and Michigan

Florida's new program and the rejected Texas and Michigan proposals assert several fallacies. By focusing on supposedly scarce "low-performing" schools, they sanctify the key elements of the governance and funding process that are responsible for the reform-resistant mess in which we find ourselves.

The focus on a particular definition of acceptable performance presumes that good and bad are black-and-white absolutes and that the government can categorize schools consistently and accurately. But there is abundant evidence that quite often things are both good and bad, depending on who is being served. Probably everyone shuns some businesses that other people cherish. Products that some people like are often disliked by others. For example, someone must love sushi bars, but I'm not going near them. Even super sushi is not for me. People differ in many ways, so no matter what criteria the state uses to measure performance, schools deemed acceptable will still serve many children badly.

The presumption that one size can fit all means that the aim of such programs is to improve schools—to push them above some minimum standard—rather than to serve the interests of every child as well as possible. We abuse or shortchange most children unless their parents can pick from a menu of specialized alternatives.

The Florida program and the Texas and Michigan proposals personify the ends-means confusion that school taxes belong to public schools rather than to children. The vouchers are worth much less than the per-child spending levels of public schools, and they are available only under appalling circumstances. The low-performing schools keep approximately half of the money that taxpayers have earmarked for a departed child's education. The parental choice granted to victims of years of certified education malpractice is meaningful only if an available, less well-funded private school can serve them better, even though the voucher users probably start far behind their new classmates. And choice opponents cite public-school returnees as evidence of the ineffectiveness of parental choice programs. But many children go back to their assigned public school because they were academically too far behind their new private-school classmates, because bad habits (such as poor discipline) developed in the public school were a problem, or because the private school running on much less money per child wasn't that much better than the assigned public school.

Privately funded choice programs typically suffer from conflicting goals. They seek to maintain broad political support, help as many children as limited funds allow, and build support for broader, publicly funded choice programs.[22] The pursuit of broad political support forces the program's sponsors to soft-pedal their goal of universal, publicly funded choice. Program sponsors emphasize their goal of helping disadvantaged children. To help as many children as possible, the programs typically offer small, partial tuition vouchers to qualifying low-income families. Because their total funding is small, privately funded programs reach only a small fraction of their applicants and a much smaller fraction of each region's K–12 population. Because of this limited reach and the small amount of funding per child, the private programs cannot create enough economic or political pressure to transform the current system. Program participants gain access to a better item on the current menu, but the menu stays the same. Like the tiny publicly funded programs, studies of typical private programs can demonstrate only whether applicants can determine consistently if an existing choice—a very inexpensive private school—is better for their child than the much better funded neighborhood public school.

To demonstrate how parental choice can transform a system, the sponsors of the private programs would have to pool their resources and establish a permanent, universal voucher program somewhere. Pursuit of the demonstration goal would mean directly helping fewer children than their current spending policy does. That the new strategy would confront major economic and political difficulties doesn't alter the economic requirements of a valid demonstration program. The vouchers have to be large enough that competition would prompt many schools to accept them as nearly full payment. And parents must be free to supplement the voucher funds so that schools can offer services that cost more than the voucher amount. Such a program would evoke a much different market response than the current programs involving partial tuition vouchers limited to a few low-income families.

To some extent, private-voucher sponsors established such a program through the ten-year effort begun in 1998–99 in the Edgewood District of San Antonio, Texas. Time will tell if the differences between the Edgewood program and the ideal conditions described here are inconsequential or significant and whether the political consequences are hugely beneficial, irrelevant, or devastating. As in the other voucher programs, only low-income families are eligible. However, unlike the other programs, there is no numerical cap—only an Edgewood District residency requirement. Because 96 percent of the district's thirteen thousand students qualify as low-income, voucher access is nearly universal (data from Walsh 1999b).[23]

Several factors may stifle or mute the expansions, school start-ups, and specialization in the Edgewood area that we would expect in a newly established competitive education industry. In the 1997–98 school year, the year prior to the initiation of the voucher program, taxpayers spent $5,820 per child enrolled in an Edgewood public school. Because the private-voucher maximum of $4,000[24] is less than the taxpayer support of $5,820 per public-school student, the vouchers do not offset fully the taxpayer discrimination against private-school users. The voucher amount is enough to cover fully the tuition of most of the area's current private schools, but because the church-run schools that dominate the private sector typically receive subsidies from the church, the vouchers may only eliminate excess capacity. The voucher amount may not be enough to induce much expansion. Parents can use the vouchers at schools that charge more than the voucher amount, but the low-income eligibility criterion will limit the ability to "add on"—that is, to supplement the voucher funds with their own money. Of most immediate relevance to private-sector growth is education entrepreneurs' willingness to respond to a program that will last only ten years. So far, there are six new schools; relatively small enterprises located in converted rented space. If the Edgewood situation is too far from being a truly competitive education industry, the private sector will not change much more during the program's five remaining guaranteed years.

If Edgewood contains enough of the key elements of a competitive education industry, the private sector will grow significantly, even if the public sector produces competitive services. The public-school share of K–12 will decrease because the population is too diverse for a single producer of anything to capture competitively a market share such as public schools' 88 percent share of K–12 education.

Universal choice in an entire medium-size county would be better than in a small part of a large urban area, as is the case with the Edgewood program. And an indefinite funding commitment is important. However, private programs have inherent limitations that will skew outcomes in potentially unpredictable ways. Uncertainty about the financial staying power of the private donors will deter some school start-ups and expansions.

Charter Schools

Charter school legislation is often seen as an experiment and as a potential reform tool. Because the alleged virtue of charter schools is their exemption from some regulations, passage of charter school legislation is an admission that the political nature of the current funding and governance process may be the source of the school system's persistent shortcomings. The political process and public institutions unfortunately are inseparable. This relationship is made apparent already by the fact that many charter schools don't control their finances and that complicated accountability formulas are considered as important as parental choice and satisfaction. Because charter schools are the largest and most rapidly growing manifestation of parental choice in action, I regret that I agree with Quentin Quade's conclusion that such schools "can be a detour, and a devastatingly bad one"(1996, 158).

The expected independence of charter schools is largely an illusion. Harvard's Caroline Hoxby has said that charter schools simply amount to new school districts. Sarah Tantillo, founder of the Charter School Resource Center, says, "I have yet to meet a regulation that charters are free from." (Pfaff, 2000) Indeed, the preliminary evidence indicates that the charter ideal of an autonomous public school is a fantasy (Finn et al. 1997; Goenner 1996; Schnaiberg 1997, 1998; Toch 1998). It's a fantasy even in states such as Arizona and Michigan, which have the "strongest" charter school laws.

A family is lucky to have a single charter alternative to its assigned school, and that option is also government controlled and lacks many of the critical freedoms and pressures of a competitive market. The option to return to a forsaken neighborhood public school does not create market forces such as price change, profit and loss, or the entreprenuerial freedom to respond by entering or exiting the K–12 education system. Opportunities to adjust prices are nonexistent, and relatively few firms run for-profit charters. Many states limit the number of charter schools, and entry always requires an approved sponsor's support. Open admission requirements create uncertainty and hinder specialization.

Charter schools may make things worse by destroying what little is left of the private sector. The private sector's primary difficulty is unequal access to resources, a problem that charter schools worsen by recruiting some of the children who would have attended private schools. Urban League president Hugh Pearson (1996) has said that private schools for black children often have to become charter schools. The November 1998 issue of *School Reform News* reported that charter schools are "killing private schools" (*School Reform* News, 1998, 12). Edgar Huffman of Phoenix said his school faced a financial disaster three years ago after he lost half of his students, a year after passage of charter school legislation. Huffman converted his school to a charter. "We basically had no choice but to go charter," he says (ibid). In the twenty-five states that do not permit private schools to convert to charters, loss of students eventually means extinction.[25]

Charters raise the government's share of K–12 and may permanently preempt the competitive education industry that would produce much greater improvement in the school system. Because charter schools do not receive public funds for capital, charter users suffer discrimination in the way private-school users do, though to a lesser extent. Charters still suffer many of the shortcomings of traditional public schools, and they will displace some private schools and shrink enrollments at others. Moreover, traditional neighborhood public schools' financial advantage may keep charters from prompting much change in the public-school system. Charter schools don't even have to outperform traditional public schools directly. A popular specialty area will attract students.

Tax Credits

Concerns about regulation (discussed at greater length later) have led some choice advocates to favor nonrefundable tax credits[26] rather than vouchers or refundable tax credits as a funding mechanism. Tax credits are seen as less amenable to regulation because the recipient keeps some of his own money rather than receiving "government" funds. Andrew Coulson's (2001) proposal, for example, offers parents a nonrefundable income tax credit for private-school expenditures. In addition, because nonrefundable tax credits don't help parents who pay little or no income tax, Coulson's proposal would also give a nonrefundable tax credit to any individual or organization (including a corporation) that donates to a privately funded low-income voucher program.[27]

Such tax credits would fill up existing private schools, but would they transform the system? I doubt it. The nonrefundable tax credit would not change significantly the precarious financial circumstances of private schools that keep their market share small. Real competition—contestability—requires nondiscrimination by the government. Public funds must support all children equally.

Consider how limited the actual tax credits would be. According to the Coulson proposal, families might earn a credit for qualifying state (not federal) tax liabilities up to half the per student cost of their local public schools. But how many families have direct state (or even combined state and local) tax liabilities anywhere near that amount for even one child? I live in Texas, where there is no state income tax. I paid approximately $3,000 last year in school property tax. It seems unlikely that any credit would fully offset all my property tax. Thus, the largest tax credit I might hope for would be significantly less than half the cost of educating one child in the public sector. Credits of that size cannot prompt system transformation. Even if a tax credit proposal were extended to federal income taxes, most taxpayers would not earn much of a credit because the income tax falls primarily on the rich. More than half of all federal income tax is paid by just 5 percent of the population. Fifty percent of American households pay almost no federal income tax. The amount of money that a household would actually save would depend heavily on income—a major political and economic liability.

The major impact of the nonrefundable educational tax credit would come through additional funding—especially through corporate charity—for private-voucher programs. It seems likely, however, that limits on the maximum credit would severely limit expansion. Arizona's "scholarship" tax credit, for example, is $500. Coulson presents an optimistic scenario suggesting that this program might eventually fund $75 million in annual low-income vouchers. At first glance, this amount seems significant, but even if all the money goes to schools (i.e., none is lost in administration and so on), it is still only enough to offer $3,000 vouchers to twenty-five thousand students; less than 3 percent of Arizona's nearly nine hundred thousand public-school students.[28] Even with a much larger credit, neither the size of the voucher nor the number of students would be large enough to unleash market forces. Low-income families with little ability to supplement a voucher will have to choose between a public-school system that has served them badly and the cheapest private schools.

Although I would make some adjustments, I do not oppose such credits.[29] The Coulson proposal would allow many families to move their children to better schools. It's an escape hatch, and I'm not against escape hatches as long as their limitations are recognized widely. They are stopgap measures to minimize the damage done by the current system while efforts to implement a true reform catalyst continue.

Competition and system transformation through market forces means more than making the private sector more affordable. It means removing the financial disadvantages that distort school choice decisions. The tax credit would not change significantly the fact that the precarious financial circumstances of private schools keep their market share small. Real competition—contestability—requires nondiscrimination by the government.

6

What Sidetracked Choice Advocacy?

The modern voucher debate began with Milton Friedman's 1955 proposal that was first read widely in chapter six of his 1962 book *Capitalism and Freedom*. He proposed that "parents who choose to send their children to private schools would be paid a sum equal to the estimated cost of educating a child in a public school" (1962, 93)—in effect, a universal voucher or refundable tax credit proposal that does not discriminate against private-school users. Friedman was not trying to shift the worst victims of the status quo to another part of the system. He argued that turning the allocation of public K–12 funds over to parents would allow product differentiation and introduce competition, which would make the school system much more efficient. And it would end the unfair treatment of private-school users.

The voucher concept enjoyed enormous initial popularity. "Liberal" scholars were especially enthusiastic about the general idea: "In the late 1960s, educational vouchers were generally regarded as a progressive proposal" and "All liberal faculty members would wish to be associated with it [education vouchers]" (Senator Patrick Moynihan qtd. in Kirkpatrick 1999, 9). So what shifted the voucher debate from Milton Friedman's simple reform proposal to complicated and limited programs that move only a few children within the system? Each set of voucher proponents unfortunately had its own unique, strongly held views about how the devil could emerge from poorly conceived details (Center for the Study of Public Policy 1970; Cohen and Farrar 1977; Coons and Sugarman 1978; Friedman 1962; Jencks 1966; Levin 1968, 1992; Rand Coporation 1977; Salganik 1981; Sizer and Whitten 1968; West 1967). Everyone found devils in everyone else's details. The voucher concept was popular, but no specific proposal was. The Friedman proposal has few details, and the details subsequently invented were a major evolutionary step in the wrong direction.

The invention and discussion of details transformed the voucher concept from a simple substitute for the current governance and funding system into an addition to it. That transformation of the voucher idea helped opponents depict voucher programs as raids on public schools and as new costs that would lead to tax increases. The scarlet "V" was born. The widely held presumption that voucher programs would be only additions to the existing funding and governance system led eventually to assertions that a voucher program would increase a school system's expenses by up to 25 percent, perhaps more (Levin and Driver 1997).[30]

Voucher became a word that many choice advocates avoid as much as possible (Fox 1977; Kronholz 2000; "School Reform Blooms" 1999). Vague and misleading substitute terms such as *school choice* and *scholarship* further confuse the public debate and reduce the likelihood that an actual program will establish market forces. And the post-Friedman proposals, including the few that became actual programs, unfortunately amounted to limited escape hatches.[31] Such programs can't transform the system through competition or by any other means, though much of the discussion still pretends that they are potential reform catalysts.

Equity concerns dominated the voucher proposals that followed during the 1960s and 1970s. Because there are no standard definitions or formulas, the focus on equity greatly complicated voucher discussions. Equity typically meant income redistribution beyond the amount inherent in the taxes that raise money for K–12.[32] Many reform advocates also wanted to grant (and still do) poor families a disproportionate share of the revenues.

In addition, the gap between the educational opportunities available to the rich and poor seemed to be a greater concern than maximizing progress. Even though Friedman argued that the poor stood to gain much more from competition than the affluent, his proposal's indifference to potential gains by the wealthy created the belief that voucher programs should be reconfigured to deny the wealthy any benefits. For example, in an influential 1970 report from the Center for the Study of Public Policy (CSPP), John Coons and Stephen Sugarman recommended a ban on add-ons and greater funding for the disadvantaged so that disadvantaged children would gain relative to affluent children. The CSPP report did not recognize that add-on bans torpedo market forces (recall that a ban on add-ons amounts to a price control) or that market forces play a critical role in improving the system for all. Furthermore, the CSPP report did not recognize that discouraging private spending on schooling might diminish directly the gains for all children or that the losses for affluent children might exceed the gains for disadvantaged children.

In the 1960s and 1970s, concerns about racial diversity were especially compelling reasons to oppose or limit parental choice. Concern that racial homogeneity would be many parents' top priority led to a sense of distrust that still exists, even though area-based public-school admissions foster de facto segregation. Parental choice today is actually a tool for racial integration because demand for specialized services often surpasses interest in student body homogeneity. But concern that programmatic interests will not adequately suppress racism or in the right proportions restricts parental choice to public-school choice that the authorities can control. Magnet school programs and other forms of "controlled" public-school choice—such as the program in Cambridge, Massachusetts—aim to create racially heterogeneous student bodies. However, the authorities often deny parental choices and substitute their own preferences. Public schools' inability to specialize to nearly the extent that would result from market forces minimizes the integration benefits of public-school choice, but at least it also reduces the scope of the mismatches between student and school characteristics that occur when the authorities veto parental choices and substitute their own. Tony Wagner, a Cambridge resident and prominent educator, confirms my pessimism about the potential for specialization by public schools: "The majority of the thirteen [Cambridge K–8 schools] seem virtually interchangeable and are mediocre" (1996, 71). Furthermore, Wagner found that "School choice has not produced significant improvements in the schools," a statement that illustrates the limited potential of restriction-laden choice and the political risks of lumping diverse programs under the general "school choice" heading and of applauding every program enthusiastically without qualification.

The confusion that grew out of the competing, complicated, restriction-laden plans no doubt contributed to the huge electoral defeats of parental choice ballot initiatives. People tend to vote against things they do not understand. The wide margins of defeat convinced many choice advocates to lower their expectations, which led to futile attempts to appease choice opponents. And advocates celebrate and support every promise to give anyone another choice, even if it might delay or jeopardize more meaningful reforms. Choice advocates typically hype every program as a choice experiment, even though no existing program can show how choice might prompt reform. An incremental strategy has evolved that basically assumes that any extra choices will unleash irresistible pressures leading to a gradual repeal of restrictions until a version of "full school choice" evolves. For many choice advocates, "full school choice" sadly can still contain many key restrictions. For example, one strong voice for reform, the *School Reform News,* called the restriction-laden Milwaukee program a working model of "full school choice" (Clowes 1998).

Chester Finn and Rebecca Gau claim that adequate choices are at hand or that we're moving there quickly and that all that is needed is a slight increase in the accessibility of current private schools. "For all the noise around vouchers, public dollars already underwrite private school attendance in a variety of ways" (1998, 79). Every use of tax money, however trivial, that makes private schools more affordable is called a "virtual voucher." Finn and Gau ignore big differences between where we are—with scattered, tiny "virtual vouchers"—and a true universal choice program that would unleash market forces. Indeed, Finn and Gau do not mention competition, not even as an important force, much less as an objective.

Because an incremental strategy is vague, slow, and even a little deceptive by definition, the strategists can deceive themselves. Many seem to have done so. Through the passage of time, changes in leadership, and slow progress, many choice advocates seem to have forgotten every goal but the ones they might achieve quickly. Despite the potentially terrible consequences of short-term pragmatism, it is easy to sympathize with such thinking. The view from the trenches is often quite limited. The fog of war forces the combatants to focus on the struggles at hand, and it obscures linkages between current and future battles.

Such confusion is typical among those who believe that they are well informed, so we are lucky that they are rare. A 1999 poll found that "a vast majority of the American public claims to have little or no knowledge about charter schools, education vouchers, or for-profit schools" (Education Policy Institute 1999). According to Terry Moe (2001), 65 percent of the American public have never heard of school vouchers. That's good because it is much easier to inform people than to dispel their misconceptions. That the semi-informed faction seems to believe in the "escape hatch," "addition to the current system" definition of parental choice is a big enough problem.

Most of the activists and K–12 analysts I encounter speak and write on this issue as if the tiny, restriction-laden current programs are legitimate, ultimately informative, or catalytic "experiments." That is certainly the media mindset. One example is a *Wall Street Journal* front-page article on the conflicting interpretations of test score data from Milwaukee's voucher users. It included this incredible statement: "Education scholars were hoping the Milwaukee experiment would finally settle whether vouchers help poor kids academically" (Davis 1996, A1),[33] a recurring plea that speaks volumes about persistent, deeply ingrained misperceptions of voucher uses and parental choice issues. Voucher systems are seen widely as only additions to the current system, a way to allow a few low-income children to attend private schools—because the system supposedly serves only poor children badly. Based on the recent expansion of Milwaukee's still restriction-laden program, the *Wall Street Journal* proclaimed that the "choice debate is over" ("Choice Debate" 2000). Choice is working as a limited escape hatch in a few places, so the debate is over? Though it would be tragic, they may be right. The persistently narrow scope of the parental choice debate may harden the public's view of parental choice enough so that policymakers use small parental choice programs only selectively as an escape hatch.

Key Elements of a Competitive Education Industry

Several previous sections made the distinction between choice that creates some limited rivalry and choice that establishes the market forces that deliver most of the goods and services we consume. This section explains in more detail why genuine competition is more effective than potential rivalry or limited actual rivalry. Giving people options doesn't necessarily foster competition or even limited rivalry. And limited rivalry can produce negative effects, especially when it occurs between a dominant producer, small rivals, and potential newcomers. For example, the MPS reaction to vouchers was an effort "to strangle the choice experiment in its crib" (McGroarty 1996, 85). Because public school systems have an average market share of 88 percent, dirty tricks such as "intimidation and misinformation" (Hess, Maranto, and Milliman 1999) can pay off. When perpetrators of underhanded behavior have huge market shares, they benefit from such behavior by picking up most of their victim's lost customers.

Contestability and Nondiscrimination

In a truly competitive setting, market share is fully contestable, the government doesn't discriminate, and flexible prices reflect constantly changing market forces. Fully contestable means that no one has an assurance of market share and that more than marginal adjustments in market share are at stake. The universally tiny market shares that some textbooks say maximize the benefits of competition[34] are likely for K–12—except in sparsely populated areas—but they are not essential. Contestability—new firms can contest market share easily—is the critical element. Economists have shown that contestability with only a few sellers at any one time still yields reasonably competitive behavior (Baumol, Panzar, and Willig 1982; Borenstein 1992; Morrison and Winston 1987).

Informed and mobile consumers are a key element of contestability. But mobility and possession of information need not be universal. We know from research and personal experience that competitive industries contain many poorly informed, low-mobility participants. I do not know much about the relative merits of different microprocessors, serial buses, and video cards. I benefit from the actions of knowledgeable consumers when I buy a computer. In other areas, poorly informed consumers benefit from my knowledge and interest. For effective competition to exist, there just have to be enough well-informed and mobile people to affect the sellers' financial viability.

Price Change

Price change is the other critical element. Schools must be free to charge whatever they want without worrying about jeopardizing the parents' eligibility for direct government support or indirect support through vouchers or tax credits. Efficiency requires that prices reflect changing production costs and consumer priorities. Price change maintains the balance between supply and demand, and it is through temporarily higher prices that rising demand prompts the appropriate supply increase. The price hike is usually temporary because the resulting rise in profitability sows the seeds of its own destruction. Higher profits motivate expansions and an influx of new producers. The influx lowers prices, returns profits to more typical levels, and prevents overexpansion.

The current education system lacks the critical price movement process because the 88 percent of K–12 children who attend public schools pay a tuition price of zero. Many existing voucher programs and prominent proposals unfortunately curb price change by forbidding private schools to cash vouchers unless they accept them as full payment.

Many prominent choice advocates and conservatives (I prefer not to name them) are too willing to accept a ban on add-ons. Some even actively support them. This is one of the few issues in which the instincts of freedom-loving choice advocates are not good enough. To succeed, we need a deep appreciation for the role of prices in market economies. Price change is not an optional part of the market mechanism. It *is* the market mechanism. Price movement regulates market participation, including how many businesses participate in each market, how they specialize, and how they change over time. For example, higher prices are often necessary to motivate as well as pay for research, development, and the costly early stages of a product's life cycle. Price flexibility—permission to add on—is a nonnegotiable element of system transformation through parental choice.

The critical add-on issue deserves much more attention. Because of the importance of the add-on option, I want to review the example I provided earlier. A tax-funded voucher worth $3,000 means that $3,000 worth of private schooling would cost a family nothing beyond the taxes they already pay. But if families cannot combine their own money with the government subsidy (i.e., add on), $3,001 worth of instruction would cost a family $3,001 more than $3,000 worth of instruction. A huge change in cost to buy a little more amounts to a price (tuition) ceiling at the taxpayer-funded amount. Universal parental choice without the right to add on would wipe out mid-price-range formal schooling options. It would limit private spending to after-school programs, tutoring, and premium schooling (i.e., elite prep schools). For example, with a $3,000 no-add-ons-allowed voucher there probably wouldn't be any $4,000 services and very few $7,000 services. Many of the families who would be willing to buy the $7,000 services by supplementing the $3,000 voucher with $4,000 of their own money would not pay the full $7,000 themselves if add-ons were not allowed. Instead of paying an extra $7,000 for an additional $4,000 worth of schooling, many parents would settle for less schooling of lower quality than they actually want and for which they are willing to pay.

Add-on bans—price controls—stifle experimentation and innovation. The opportunity to charge high prices for innovative practices is an important incentive. In addition, high initial prices may be necessary. New practices and products are often costly. Wealthy individuals' purchases of new goods such as DVD players, cell phones, and computers often sustain such innovations until experience and competition drive prices and costs down enough to make former luxuries the norm.

The right to add on also promotes responsible shopping, and it is arguably a simple matter of fairness. Why should parents lose their child's share of public funds just because they want to do more for their own child than can be done for every child?

Additional schooling for affluent children doesn't make less-affluent children worse off. Society benefits when the affluent devote their earnings to the education of their children. Attempts to go beyond the appropriate and feasible level of equal public funding (a high minimum level of education opportunity)—to equalize gains rather than to maximize them—have few if any equity benefits and high efficiency costs. The trade-offs are severe. The wealthy are always going to have advantages. Efforts to minimize such advantages will torpedo key market forces and distort the political process. Programs that target the poor are inevitably poor programs.[35]

Discussion

Contestability also requires a high degree of certainty about underlying authority and demand. Shaky political support for the key elements of the market or a credible basis for a legal challenge will discourage potential K–12 entrepreneurs. Temporary programs and those that rely on donations will not stimulate major invest-ments. Temporary and shaky programs also reduce parental inter-est. Parents value continuity. They are less likely to use a school if its survival depends on political decisions that have no relationship to school quality or parent preferences. Some of the recent charter closures are good examples of such decisions.

Competition is mistakenly thought to be part of many scenar-ios that are far from competitive. A key area I have not mentioned yet is the growing trend toward contracting out to businesses the management of chronically low-performing public schools, a form of limited privatization. Many public schools certainly are managed badly, but changing a government-operated monopoly into a gov-ernment-regulated private monopoly offers few long-term benefits. An opportunity to profit by doing better than predecessors is a sig-nificant incentive, but the school system still lacks the market forces (contestability, nondiscrimination, and price change) needed to bring about continuous long-term improvement. Further, the con-tract may restrict the firm's options. Changes in politically sensitive areas such as personnel and curriculum may be off-limits. In addi-tion, attendance-area policies may prevent the spread of any short-term improvements that result from the pressure to outperform a low-performing predecessor. Nearby schools don't have to emulate successful practices in order to keep their students.

In addition, the lack of direct competition for students, the need to produce some quick results, and uncertainty about contract renewal can produce counterproductive behavior. Uncertainty about contract renewal tempts firms to maximize short-term profits by cutting corners or to neglect important instructional tasks in favor of items related to media spin and contract renewal. Underinvestment is likely because the management contract might not last long enough to recover investment outlays.

To close this section, I want to repeat that, rhetoric and media hype notwithstanding, the modest voucher, tax credit, and public-school choice programs (including charter schools) widely touted as experiments lack nearly all of the key requirements for competition.[36] They move only a relatively few children, mostly among existing schools; leave the broken system intact and sanctify its key elements; and mislead observers as to the nature of the real K–12 problem—a low-performing system, not isolated low-performing schools.

7

Loose Lips Sink Causes

I'm not against the current limited programs. They help a few children, with little or no risk to those who remain in their neighborhood public school. The impact of tiny choice programs on unsubsidized private-school users remains uncertain. If it is negative, it must be small, or the school owners would refuse to admit the voucher users. Those aspects of limited choice programs deserve systematic analysis. What I object to and strongly criticize is the excessive amount of attention such programs receive and the wrong, misleading, and irrelevant statements made about them, especially when such statements come from choice advocates.

Empirical Evidence

The conversion of assorted trustworthy numbers into relevant data sets, the conversion of data into evidence, and the interpretation of evidence are challenging under the best of circumstances. The parental choice debate compounds those challenges with political pressure to choose particular data sets, to adjust analysis strategies (model specification), and to interpret findings in a way that advances a cause. Bias is certain. Distortion is likely. There is already plenty of both and surely much more to come. Therefore, it is impossible to be too careful in how we determine which situations can generate useful evidence.

Many prominent choice advocates are careless. They attach the term *experiment*—the typical label for any situation that will produce evidence—to almost every situation in which a new option is created formally (Sawhill and Shannon 1998).[37] Choice advocates' newsletters describe the alleged evidence of the benefits of even tiny doses of choice, without any caveats. They rarely mention the debilitating impact of the restrictions, the absence of competition, and the mistaken focus on helping a few children rather than on improving the entire school system.

None of the current programs justify headlines such as Paul Peterson's "A Report Card on School Choice" (1997), newsletters with titles proclaiming "School Vouchers on Trial in Milwaukee and Cleveland" (1998), the title *The Market Approach to Education* (Witte 2000) for a book about the early years of the Milwaukee program, or statements such as Daniel McGroarty's that choice advocates (disciples of "theoretical models that borrow from free market economics") can "test their theories against the reality of the one city [Milwaukee] where it [competition] exists" (1996). It is definitely not the case that "these educational choice initiatives [i.e., tiny existing programs] are based on the free-market principle that competition and consumer choice produce excellence in educational services" (Salisbury 1997, 1).

Alan Bonsteel said that the Milwaukee program was an experiment "in a system of open competition and freedom of choice in education" and that it was "modeled after the highly successful GI Bill of Rights" (Bonsteel and Bonilla 1997, 5), even though the GI Bill is a much more open, larger, and less-restrictive choice program. Jerry Hume claimed that the Milwaukee program was "a big step in the direction" of accountability to education consumers (1990, 55). Jeanne Allen, president of the Center for School Reform, argued that the Milwaukee program had to produce noteworthy academic and equity gains or "two of the key arguments of choice proponents would be refuted" (*Washington Times* November 10, 1993). Each claim was based on the tiny, restriction-laden, pre-expansion Milwaukee program. Sadly, such misstatements are quite common.

The heated debate over voucher student achievement threatens to render competition politically infeasible. Even the expanded Milwaukee program would not justify general headlines about the usefulness of parental choice as a reform catalyst. Choice opponents "spin" their findings about the same limited programs into their favorite general conclusion that parental choice is a failed reform (Drury 2000). Both sides ignore disclaimers such as John Witte's statement that "this program should not be used as evidence for evaluating more inclusive choice programs" (Witte, Bailey, and Thorn 1993, 29; see also Testa and Surya 1999). Indeed, as the title of his recent book—*The Market Approach to Education* (2000)—demonstrates, Witte eventually ignored it himself.

Economists—scholars who study market forces—are among those so eager for something to analyze that they lower their standards regarding what is worth analyzing or forget their own disclaimers about the kinds of conclusions the data will support. Even the best available data usually have severe limitations. Many parental choice advocates and studies don't recognize that problem. A 1997 article published in a peer-reviewed economics journal contains several good examples. It surveys existing parental choice studies and draws its own conclusions (Lamdin and Mintrom 1997). Even though there is virtually no resemblance between the universal voucher plan that Milton Friedman proposed and the privately financed, partial-tuition vouchers currently available to a few low-income families in a few cities, the authors of the survey equate them! "The nature of some of these [privately financed voucher] programs allows for studies of essentially Friedman-like voucher arrangements" (235). In effect, the authors allege that a partial tuition voucher for a few low-income families—a tiny fraction of the student population in an area—would establish nondiscrimination, price movement, and contestability in the whole system (Friedman's proposal). No way! Two of the papers presented at the prestigious February 2001 Conference on the Economics of School Choice exceeded their data's limitations. Both assumed that data produced by the current system might inform a discussion of the full spectrum of parental choice possibilities. Thomas Nechyba (2001) assumed that a parental choice proposal that established competition would not change the way instruction is delivered, but that just the extensive specialization produced by competitive pressure would change drastically the way schools operate. Caroline Hoxby (2001) claimed that the current system—high barriers to choice and relative school uniformity notwithstanding—reveals some significant, broadly generalizable effects of choice. "Evidence from the traditional forms of choice [decide to pay tuition or not, and pick a school by picking a home] can reveal the long-term, general equilibrium effects of choice."

When Schools Compete: A Cautionary Tale (Fiske and Ladd 2000) is another incredible example of choice advocates' carelessness. Duke economist Helen Ladd coauthored the study of New Zealand's policy of universal choice among government-operated schools. The New Zealand situation that is the focus of the book was so thoroughly researched and reported that the authors discredit their own conclusions, including the conclusion embodied in the title of the book. There are no profits and no market-determined prices, there is extensive central control of instructional practices, and 96.5 percent of the children attend the government-owned schools. New Zealand does not have anything close to real competition. The central government controls the supply of schools, and there is no way to contest market share. In a market environment, copycat entrepreneurs relieve overcrowding at popular schools by imitating popular practices. But in New Zealand, crowding persists because the government refuses to "invest in new school facilities while others [schools] remain underutilized" (250). The government does not close or reconstitute unpopular schools. Instead, the government forces families to use schools they want to flee, either by leaving them no alternative or by reestablishing attendance zones. Specialization is minimal because "local goals were secondary to those imposed from the center in the form of the National Education Guidelines" (298). Enrollment (customer choice) is only one determinant of each school's funding. Ladd documents the absence of market forces, but makes statements such as "New Zealand's foray into the realm of *full parental choice and competition*" (250, emphasis added), "a system of parental choice and *market competition*" (292, emphasis added), and "self-governing schools functioning in a competitive environment" (297). New Zealand's real cautionary tale is one that demonstrates the effects of limited choice when competition is absent.

Economist Scott Milliman states that Arizona's charter school law "initiated a free market in public education" (Maranto and Milliman 1999, A25). But the state regulates market entry; charters and their "competitors" are accountable to the same public officials. Traditional public-school districts enjoy preferential funding. Charters must fund capital investments out of the per-pupil funds that traditional public schools can allocate fully to operations. Milliman says that charter schools are "market driven," even though they are almost exclusively nonprofit organizations that must accept every applicant they have space for. Charter operators can't set the price of their services, and their chief rival—traditional public schools—controls more than 80 percent of the "market." The error is common. In a Brookings Institution panel discussion (February 24, 2000), Helen Ladd claimed that charter schools are "a market-based reform strategy" (based on Fiske and Ladd 2000). Joseph Viteritti claims that "real competition" exists with unlimited charter schools (1999, 221). Lewis Solmon, Michael Block, and Mary Gifford characterize charter schools as "A Market-Based Education System in the Making" (2000).

Journals, talk shows, and the popular press expose many misunderstandings—and some big ones belong to choice advocates. Rebuttals and corrections are rare. The misstatements reveal what many activists believe and the misinformation they communicate to policymakers and the public. Even expanded access to neighborhood public schools—public-school choice short of charter legislation— often is seen as a test of market forces. Interdistrict choice is a very weak form of choice in which the receiving district can often decline to accept the applicant. Nevertheless, David Armor authored a report titled *Competition in Education: A Case Study of Interdistrict Choice* (1997), and G. Carl Ball uses phrases such as "market-driven," "the competitive way," and "provide the customer the opportunity to evaluate the competition" (1990, 54–55) to describe public-school choice—that is, choice among different branches of the same producer. Tom Peters says that public-school choice is "a surrogate for competition" (1990, 57). In 1986, the National Governors Conference issued a statement endorsing "the concept of public school choice as a way to unlock the values of competition in the marketplace" (Viteritti 1999, 57). In a Joe Nathan book, *Public Schools by Choice* (1989), Adam Urbanski says, "Competition among public schools would be more fair and more productive than competition between public and private schools" (228). In the same book, Herbert Walberg complains about bureaucracies "unsubjected to market competition" and then suggests that choice limited to the schools owned and run by the government education bureaucracy will solve that problem (68). John Chubb and Terry Moe say that "district- or state-wide open enrollment systems and magnet schools" (1990a, 21) would achieve meaningful competition. Their controversial, widely read book *Politics, Markets, and America's Schools* (1990b) argues convincingly that bureaucracy significantly inhibits educational achievement and that bureaucracy is an inherent part of democratic control. Then, in the final chapter of this book, the authors lobby for a choice program run by a bureau in a democratically elected government.[38] They believe a "market system" is perfectly consistent with bureaucratic control of the choices, including price controls. And John Witte and Mark Rigdon argue that the Chubb and Moe plan would mean "complete autonomy for all schools" (1993, 95).

There's not nearly enough effort to curb the intellectual dumbing-down of competitive education systems. Economists could develop models of competitive scenarios such as the Milton Friedman proposal and then compare the predicted effects of it to the status quo and to the predicted effects of the restriction-laden proposals that are often mislabeled market experiments. But they don't. Economists such as Masato Aoki and Susan Feiner (1996) as well as Dennis Epple and Richard Romano (1998) have modeled prominent proposals similar to the Chubb and Moe plan (1990b, last chapter), but they fail to point out the fact that these proposals lack real competition. These omissions contribute to the dangerously narrow focus of the parental choice debate.

Because of the current distorted view of market forces, and because limited programs can deliver significant benefits to the few who directly participate, escape-hatch programs are likely to spread. New York City's former mayor Rudolph Giuliani proposed a Milwaukee-style low-income voucher program for New York (Walsh 1999a, 3). Howard Fuller argues that the positive results from Milwaukee and Cleveland mean that these programs "should be expanded to other cities" (1997, 1). Clint Bolick believes that the "Milwaukee Plan should be exported" ("Voucher Advocate" 1992). In 2000, Nina Rees, then with the Heritage Foundation,[39] said "conservative lawmakers and minority activists in Colorado plan to promote a Milwaukee-style pilot program for Denver." A front-page article in *Education Week* states that "more policymakers are borrowing a page from Florida's book and linking their choice plans to the performance of public schools" (Bowman 2000, 1). Among the additional policymakers is President George W. Bush, whose parental choice proposals focus on low-performing schools. Such minor adjustments of the status quo might stymie reform efforts.

Careless Public-Private School Comparisons

Many analysts fall into the intellectual trap of assuming that current private-school practices and outcomes are the alternative to public schools. Not so! The constraints, incentives, and available resources will be very different in a competitive education industry.

Edwin West highlights a key symptom of likely differences between the current private sector and private schools in a true market setting in his statement that "Market forces are connected with profit-seeking, but 98 percent of America's private schools are not-for-profit institutions" (1992, 423).[40] Because most public and private schools need significant improvement, the attractiveness of true reform catalysts does not depend on whether existing private schools produce better academic outcomes than existing public schools. We must aspire to a much higher standard than the performance of today's private schools, and there is considerable historical and theoretical evidence that nondiscrimination, contestability, and market-determined prices would produce enormous improvements.

Disappointing but not shocking are studies that describe the current situation and imply that the findings have wide relevance. For example, Jay Greene writes that parental choice would promote integration because in Cleveland "private schools, on average, are better integrated than are public schools" (2000, 72). And Joseph Viteritti thinks it very important that "inner-city parochial schools are more effective in meeting the educational needs of poor children than are typical public schools in the same neighborhood" (1999, 15). The statements are accurate but also misleading. To many, the clear message of such reports is that parental choice simply means giving some families better access to existing schooling alternatives.

Some analysts, including some economists, argue that the features of the current system tell us what to expect from a competitive market system. Such claims are stunning. Aoki and Feiner conclude mistakenly that the chiefly religious nature of the private sector "profoundly colors the argument for market choice" (1996). And their analysis appeared in a volume edited by two very highly respected economists.

The most shocking gaffe appears in a *Wall Street Journal* editorial by Chubb and Moe, two of the best-known and earliest choice advocates. They acknowledge that existing private schools operate with a significant handicap: "Private schools generally have smaller [per pupil] budgets than public schools." Still, they say choice advocacy is worthwhile only if existing private schools are superior to public schools: "If there are no differences between public and private schools, there is little reason to support educational choice *of any kind* (emphasis added), public or private" (1991). They ignore the debilitating effect of having to charge much more for a much less expensive service and reach that conclusion even though competition would significantly change both public and private schools. A 1996 Dan Goldhaber article on public and private high schools is a more recent, more extensive example of the same mistake.

Related to this myopia about the potential for system transformation were the frequent claims that the U.S. Supreme Court would decide the constitutionality of vouchers[41] and other forms of government payment to schools. The underlying rationale of such claims is that parental choice becomes meaningless without church participation because church-run schools dominate the private sector now. If accurate, it would mean that parental choice is already meaningless in the states with "Blaine amendments" in their constitutions. The good news is that the concern about the legality of church-run school participation has virtually no economic basis. With nondiscrimination, a secular private sector will grow to whatever market share parents desire. Secular schools' initial tiny share will just mean that it will take them a little longer to get there. Because public schools have the lion's share of classroom capacity, they will have plenty of time to make themselves choiceworthy, but they must eventually do so or become private. Competitive settings would contain public and private schools only if both could excel at something important. The bad news is that excluding churches from parental choice programs would continue the current practice of discriminating against devoutly religious taxpayers and that the policies needed to establish the competitive education industry may not be politically feasible without the support of families who prefer church-run schools.

8

Getting There: Back Up,
Then Move Forward

Changing the Debate

The evolutionary dumbing-down of parental choice from reform catalyst (Friedman) to escape hatch needs to be reversed. Debates always depend on the definition of key terms. How the public will define key terms such as *school choice, parental choice, tuition tax credit,* and *voucher program* depends greatly on what choice advocates support. Choice opponents are not going to liberalize narrow definitions of choice and voucher program participation. Failure to express reservations about restriction-laden programs fosters the perception that parental choice is just an escape hatch for disadvantaged children in especially bad schools. Choice advocates' unqualified, enthusiastic support of restriction-laden programs signals that they believe the current system serves most children well. And when programs can help only a relatively few students, many people may conclude that nonparticipants will suffer (the "vouchers are bad because they will hurt public schools" argument). Others will conclude that such modest programs have no relevance to reform efforts. For example, former education secretary Richard Riley and National Education Association general counsel Robert Chanin said the Washington, D.C., voucher proposal and the Milwaukee program affect too few students to merit public debate or funding (Cordell 1998). Top Clinton administration education officials such as Riley, Gerald Tirozzi (Tirozzi 1997), and Terry Peterson (in Danitz 1997) made that point often. Chanin said the "problems of urban school districts cannot be solved by schemes [i.e., the expanded Milwaukee program] that skim off 5,000–15,000, but leave 85,000–95,000 behind" (qtd. in Walsh 1998). New York City Schools chancellor Rudy Crew "criticized the parental choice program for serving only a tenth of the students in Milwaukee" ("Two School Chiefs" 2000, 10). Instead of saying "you're right, we need universal choice," choice advocates typically defend the restriction-laden program. Former education secretary William Bennett's response to Riley's criticism of the D.C. proposal is a good example: "It's a very odd argument that unless we can help everybody, then we will help no one" (qtd. in "Two School Chiefs" 2000, 10). Bennett didn't say why he assumed we can't help everyone. Existing public-school spending is enough to publicly fund universal choice at a very high level.

Restrictions often create more grounds for criticism than they eliminate. And the elimination of some criticisms does little to mollify the key choice opponents. As Daniel McGroarty (1998), New Mexico's Governor Gary Johnson (Rees 1999a), and others point out, key opponents (such as the teacher unions) resist every parental choice program with the same vigor. Because limited programs will face as much resistance as 100 percent child-based, nondiscriminatory public funding, it makes sense to talk about the latter almost exclusively. That would minimize the political damage that may result from the compromise-based, limited programs that cautious politicians will enact, and it avoids additional criticism. The focus on all children would clearly establish the goal of choice advocacy (reform, not limited escape). The reform goal will become increasingly attractive as it becomes better known (Moe 2001, chap. 7), and efforts to revive and improve the current system will continue to demonstrate the futility of the other approach.

To reorient the parental choice debate from escape to reform, several messages must appear often. First, we must make it clear that the current K–12 menu does not define the possible choices. Competition will create a much different private sector than the current one. Second, we must communicate the message that the current capacity of private schools only limits how many children can attend private schools in the very near term. Third, we must make it clear that programs that foster limited movement within the system cannot reveal how broader choice programs would change the system. Market forces are not an automatic result of potential rivalry. Fourth, we must emphasize that price change is a key element of competition and a cornerstone of the market mechanism. Finally, we must make the argument that real competition prompts producer specialization, which is a key to productivity, relentless pursuit of improvement, and integration. Specialization and the selectivity that must accompany it are not discrimination. We need a diverse school system with at least one great choice for every child, not a one-size-fits-all system that imagines that every child learns the same way.

We must avoid the term *experiment*. At the very least, it makes competition and choice seem like novel, risky concepts. Changing a badly broken education system does not risk much. According to the famous *A Nation at Risk* report, our current system is already producing effects that would be seen as acts of war if a foreign power were responsible. If someone says it's a gamble and urges caution, ask them which part of the current system they'd miss. Choice and competition are the norm in our economy. Lack of competition is the novel practice that demands justification. So-called pilot programs cannot generate useful data, and they have an enormous potential to create misleading data and excuse delay.

Do not assume that teachers are solid choice opponents. As high burnout and turnover rates attest, many teachers dislike the status quo, and there's every reason to believe that dedicated teachers have almost as much to gain from competition as their students do. A strategy to directly solicit teacher support for parental choice deserves much more attention.[42]

Efforts to solicit teachers indirectly through their unions are pointless. A competitive education industry would greatly diminish the power of teacher labor unions. Teacher unions in some countries support parental choice programs but only after getting used to them—and only because they are very different from enormous U.S. teacher unions such as the National Education Association and the American Federation of Teachers. Escape-hatch programs will be much more difficult to "sell" to teachers. Limited choice programs raise many concerns and offer few of the opportunities to professionalize teaching found in a competitive education industry. Debate over limited programs helps union officials slander choice and thereby harden rank-and-file opposition to it.

The Critical Policies and Key Options

I want to preface the discussion of critical policies with my political assumptions. Competition may be politically infeasible, or it can be made infeasible by trying to do it the wrong way or trying to accomplish too much at once. In part because our education system has failed to foster adequate understanding of market forces, any pro-competition coalition will be fragile with little margin for political error. Because of the political obstacles to major policy change, we need to individually address major issues such as competition, public spending level,[43] government ownership of schools, and compulsory schooling. For example, efforts to achieve competition and, say, to reduce public funding of K–12 in the same legislative package have a much lower probability of success than would an effort to achieve competition with public spending held constant at the current level. Indeed, I believe that competition will make other desirable changes possible or reveal whether they are desirable.

Here are the minimum policy requirements of a competitive education industry with the status quo as the starting point:

1. Parental choice alone decides each school's share of state and local government funding. Some people may argue that the requirement is overstated, that market forces can survive even if customer

preferences are not the only determinant of a school's instructional funding. The direct, immediate effects of having other funding determinants would be negligible, but distortions will creep in, and departures from a well-defined, easily understood equal-share standard create a slippery slope and incentives to spend resources to lobby for a larger share.

2. Equal public funding follows a child no matter who owns the school he or she attends (the key nondiscrimination principle). Comparable children in public, private nonprofit, or private for-profit schools receive the same amount of public money. Again, many people will allege that this policy essential is overstated. And the same rebuttal applies. Nondiscrimination is a well-defined standard without a stable, well-defined substitute.

3. There should be no barriers or disincentives to discourage families from spending their own money on formal schooling or on other education services such as after-school programs, summer instruction, or tutoring. Parents thus must be free to buy more schooling than public funds alone will allow, but without losing access to public funding. Their ability to do so establishes the critical price-movement component of market forces.

4. Competition must begin with state and local K–12 spending at least at the level that existed prior to the policy change that facilitated competition.

5. Federal K–12 funding should continue to provide supplemental public support to special-needs children on a case-by-case basis.

6. The government must define what constitutes a "school," including a minimum enrollment. The minimum enrollment will deter fraud and extremist schools and stop families from earning income by educating their own children. The latter may seem unnecessary, even inappropriately intrusive and counterproductive. But with public funding of $5,000 to $7,000 per child (depending on how you define total funding and what share supports administration), families might support themselves by teaching

many children at home. That possibility could cause a large increase in the population[44] along with shrinkage in the labor-force participation rate and the tax base.

7. There must be a way to verify the enrollment of each school.

Key policy options would include:

1. *The public funding mechanism.* School enrollment is the only piece of information we need to send the correct government check to each school. Direct payment based on an enrollment report is fine. That method is the simplest administratively, but it may not be constitutional for governments to pay churches *directly* even if parents independently determine the recipient of each payment. In addition, direct payments to producers suffer from regulation much more than payments to consumers. *Indirect* payment methods such as tax credits and vouchers are constitutional and may have a better chance of resisting regulation. I prefer a fully refundable tax credit. Then schools bill parents, and the government has to issue checks only to families with K–12 credits larger than their tax liabilities. Vouchers are fine, but they probably have higher administrative costs than refundable tax credits, and because of the "V-word" phenomenon discussed earlier, a voucher program will always have some political excess baggage.

2. *Age and geographical differences in the level of public funding per child.* Ending government discrimination against private-school users does not preclude age-based or place-based differences in public funding per child. Indeed, they are probably a good idea. Current private-school tuition levels indicate that it costs more to educate older children. Likewise, because salaries and living costs are not geographically uniform, it might be a good idea to fund similar children in some places at higher rates than others.

3. *Administrative spending.* I don't mean spending to support district office administrators. Districts or public schools will have

to decide how much they want to spend on a central office staff. Private-school franchises will face the same issues. By administration spending, I mean spending to administer the parental choice–based program, with the remainder of the funds sent to schools according to parents' choices. With child-based funding, the administrative requirements include enrollment verification, fund disbursal, monitoring and enforcement requirements of regulations, and fraud prevention.

Uncertainty about the outcome of the political struggle over age-based and place-based differences in funding per child and how much administrative spending will cost is another strong reason to permit add-ons. Private add-ons can keep political mischief and genuine error from doing too much damage.

4. *Government's role.* The government must determine the boundaries of its role as information provider and data generator, including standardized testing requirements and content. Test score comparisons will still matter to some parents, but with the specialization of a competitive education industry such data won't matter as much as they do with the comprehensive uniformity that now dominates public schools. Testing may become private, as the various types of specialized schools struggle to achieve highly valued, demanding certifications from professional associations and other types of accrediting entities that will probably arise for common specialization areas.[45] The government might then collect, tabulate, and distribute the private test data.

5. *The definition of a school.* States would have to define the term *school* to determine eligibility to receive public K–12 instructional funding. The definition that states use to enforce compulsory attendance laws probably will serve that purpose adequately, but there will be pressures to add regulations. Such pressures must be resisted. The market will resolve all of the other issues, including things such as personnel qualifications, textbooks, curricula, food service, and transportation services, which are competition areas. Market forces deter and punish mistakes more effectively than costly, stifling government

regulations can prevent them. Choice and tolerance, not regulation, are the answers to disagreement over what schools should teach. One reason detailed curriculum content regulations would be counterproductive is the same as the reason the demand for them—the ever-changing controversy over what the rules should require. The other reason is that they would hinder the relentless pursuit of improvement that characterizes competitive markets.

6. *The requirement that parents supplement government funds.* People choose more carefully when they spend their own money. Coulson (1999) found that the financial involvement of parents was a common denominator of effective school systems throughout history. To require parents to add on, public funding could provide X dollars per child or Y percent of tuition and fees per child, whichever is *less.* Another advantage of an add-on requirement is that it defuses arguments that public schools will have less money per student once all K–12 children share the existing K–12 dollars. However, an add-on requirement also has potential disadvantages. Because all schools would receive their public funding through parental choices, an add-on requirement would face political opposition from parents who currently do not want to move their child to a private school. Add-on requirements also require the government to monitor each school's tuition and fees.

The Question of Regulation

Direct payment, universal vouchers, and refundable tax credits are often criticized for their potential to expand private-school regulation. Because of compulsory attendance laws, states can regulate private schools already, but many choice advocates fear that even indirect state funding through vouchers or tax credits would create significant new regulation (Bast and Harmer 1997; Quade 2000).

It is true that transforming the system through a universal voucher program or a refundable tax credit might lead to more regulation of the private sector. But doing nothing might lead to more regulation of the private sector, anyway—the direction in which we have been going for over a century. There is unfortunately no magic set of institutions that guarantees freedom from regulation. The only way to fight regulation is to teach the benefits of freedom and the costs of regulation—and, of course, to maintain eternal vigilance against assaults on our liberty.

One must also bear in mind that 88 percent of the children today are already schooled in a heavily regulated system. If we don't try to transform the system, we can be sure that these children will remain trapped and poorly served. The remaining children, the ones whom further regulation threatens, are also for the most part poorly funded and *not truly experiencing the advantages of a competitive system.* I am not convinced that a refundable tax credit or fully funded voucher risks any more regulation of the private sector than exists now or will exist in the near future. But even if the risk were greater than with other approaches, the potential benefits of system transformation are worth it! Small tax credits, private voucher programs, and escape hatches cannot help the great bulk of the 88 percent who currently are stuck in the public schools.

An Implementation Example for My Proposal

Suppose a county with one hundred thousand K–12 children enacts the policy essentials described in the previous sections for the 2003–2004 school year. The payment method is a refundable tax credit. Suppose enrollment stays at one hundred thousand and that state and local public funding for K–12 stays at the $600 million spent in 2002–2003. For 2003–2004, authorities will have $600 million to fund tax credits, debt service, administrative costs, and fraud prevention. The school authorities can assign the bonded indebtedness to individual schools and force each to pay its own debt-service costs from the money paid by parents, but it may be difficult to make such an allocation. Private schools have to pay start-up costs with the money paid by parents, so a decision not to allocate school district debt to individual schools will give public schools a slight, temporary cost advantage.

Suppose that debt service consumes $50 million a year and that the administrative requirements of child-based funding, including fraud prevention, cost another $5 million. For a margin of safety in case federal funds are not enough to supplement special-needs families, the county school authorities set aside $20 million. In the first years of child-based funding, the authorities will need to allocate money for severance and retraining support. Help for educators seeking new careers or adjusting to changing K–12 opportunities would yield significant economic and political benefits. Allocating $25 million per year for this help will leave $500 million ($600 million minus $50, $5, $20, and $25 million) to fund the tax credits— an *average* of $5,000 per K–12 child ($500 million divided by one hundred thousand children). However, the money per child will probably vary by grade level, with more than $5,000 for older children and less for younger children.

Discussion

Suppose the county is typical, and 10 percent of the students attended private schools during the time when public schools had their monopoly on public funding. Child-based funding—ending the government's discrimination against private-school users—will cause a 10 percent drop in the public-school system's public funding per pupil. Even though schools can charge more than the average $5,000 public funding level, and child-based funding will eliminate some costs, some people will cite potential hardship for low-income families as a way to justify increased public spending on K–12, and they'll find ready allies in private-school operators eager for opportunities to raise their prices. Charities can eliminate that justification for more public funding by providing a low-income safety net that provides help for families who don't live near a school that will accept the approximately $5,000 in public funding as full payment and who can't afford to add on. A true scholarship program that gives low-income families access to schools that demand large add-ons would have a great deal of economic and political value as well.

Child-based funding would eliminate directly some costly tasks and would undermine the rationale for others. School budgets would depend on parents' choices, not on the decisions of the district's central office, which would significantly weaken the rationale for an expensive district superintendent and a raft of associates, assistants, directors, and program coordinators. There would be no need for district administrators to develop budgets or to maintain, adjust, or enforce school attendance areas. Government-owned schools can maintain their district identity if they want, but schools would assume many former district functions. Personnel is a good example. School principals want to hire their own staff; they don't want district administrators to do it for them.[46] Because district schools would not benefit equally from district-provided support services, the schools would increasingly resist funding them. In addition, the changes that would come with the pressure to specialize would require a wider range of service providers than most districts have or can afford to employ full-time.

Ending government discrimination against private-school users would increase the demand for private schooling. Unless education entrepreneurs and existing private-school owners have enough advance warning to provide additional capacity to handle the demand increase, the increased demand for private schooling would drive private-school tuition above the per-student public funding level, at least temporarily. Even if there is enough time to expand facilities and establish new schools, some schools will have more applicants than space. Because oversubscribed schools may not discover the problem until it is too late to change advertised prices for the upcoming school year, they will do exactly what choice opponents have warned they would—they will become more selective. Though this is exactly what choice opponents warn against—schools rather than parents exercising choice—their warning is misleading. The shortages would be short-lived. Copycat entrepreneurs would quickly offer more of the most popular services. When explaining this facet of the transition to a competitive education industry, parental choice advocates should also point out that selectivity—school choice by public-school officials rather than by parents—already exists in the current system. However, the current system contains no mechanism to quickly eliminate any space shortages in magnet schools or, in some states, charter schools.

Some people fear that private-sector growth will create a second strong lobby for higher school taxes, but what they forget is that public schools' clout will shrink far more than private-sector schools' clout might grow. A competitive education industry probably will produce weaker pressure for government funding increases as school operators will not be able to stifle the signals (such as quality improvement and excess capacity) that can justify spending restraint.

9

The Outlook

The prospects of a competitive education industry and probably the country's future depend on choice advocate unity and a consistent message. I've covered the message issues already and repeated many of them, with one exception. As we know most vividly from the difficulties in eastern Europe but also in this country through events such as California's power crisis, inattention to transition issues (adjustment behavior and its consequences) can scuttle or distort reform. Choice advocates have to avoid as many of the economic and political calamities and speed bumps as possible and prepare the public for the rest.

For example, many new schools will have controversial practices, and some badly conceived schools will fail. That raises the issue of bankruptcy, a key element of the market mechanism. Bankruptcy is an easily monitored, relatively objective indicator of failure, and the possibility of bankruptcy strengthens the incentive to pay attention to customers and to make decisions carefully. We'll have to explain that its consequences are not as terrible as some members of the public might otherwise assume. Bankruptcy may simply provide time to restructure, and we can require school operators to carry insurance against midyear shutdowns. Even when there is a change in ownership, significant dislocations of students or educators may not follow. New owners have strong incentives to cater to the existing student body's capabilities and desires. New owners will abandon the existing faculty and staff or specialty areas only where there is a clear link to the bankruptcy problem.

There will be episodes of fraud and kickbacks. Burned-out teachers and obsolete administrators too old to train for new careers will lose their jobs. We'll have to point out that change is impossible without some dislocations, and that competition doesn't make everyone into an angel.

It will take time for existing schools to develop a specialization. Until then there will be little but bad and better versions of similar schools. Everyone naturally prefers the better version. That's why student body composition currently influences more choices than it will after extensive specialization arises. Until specializations develop, the better schools will become selective, and some will raise prices; both of these actions will favor the affluent, which is still correlated with race. The choice opponents will say, "I told you so." We have to predict and explain such temporary transitional effects publicly, and counsel patience

To achieve the political unity needed to achieve a competitive education industry, choice advocates must change their focus from disagreement about the final destination (increased efficiency, equity, less government influence on K–12, complete separation of school and state) to agreement on a road that gets us much closer to that destination. The competition road leads to many final destinations, all of which are much better than the status quo. Other roads lead nowhere or are tempting detours (charter legislation, vouchers for low-performing schools or low-income families, modest tax credits) that may produce some quick benefits but forestall or substantially delay system transformation through market forces.

One symptom of our preoccupation with the controversy over final destinations and of the failure to agree on a road is some choice advocates' opposition to any plan that might increase regulation of the existing mostly resource-starved, already much endangered private sector. They support only modest tax credits such as the one described earlier or complete separation of school and state.[47] They overlook the existing financial duress that threatens the size and quality of the private sector much more than the regulation that can infect a truly competitive education industry. The "my way or no way" attitude helps preserve a system in which nearly 90 percent of children attend schools that cannot be more regulated. They surely would enjoy greater freedom under any version of a truly competitive education industry, and the current governance process probably will increase the regulation of the private 10 percent anyway. Existing compulsory attendance laws provide states all the authority they need. The restriction-laden choice programs that are likely to spread in the absence of a dramatic broadening of the current debate, combined with the legitimate fear of extinction that many private schools have, will expand regulation of private schools much more than a competitive education industry might.

10

Conclusion

Fallacies and the pursuit of political expediency have dumbed down school choice advocacy. School choice proponents do little but pursue and defend escape hatches from the very worst schools of a bad system. We can do better. We must achieve a system that does not discriminate against private-school users and does not impede market forces with price caps and other regulations.

Though the route to the competition road is lined with misleading signs and strewn with land mines, we should be optimistic for several major reasons. Key parts of the opposition coalition, such as low-income groups and teachers, have much to gain from system transformation; the former already recognize this fact and are putting increased pressure on their leaders to fall into line, and the growing difficulty of recruiting and retaining teachers may be what ultimately forces an overhaul of the K–12 system.

The greatest threats to progress are low expectations and misleading alleged experiments. We need to achieve real competition in only one reasonably populous area to assure that eventually it will exist virtually everywhere. If we keep our eyes on the goal and are not distracted by half-measures and by worse than half-measures, it can happen quickly, much like the sudden collapse in 1989 of the socialist regimes of eastern Europe. Even the political worst-case scenario can only delay competition. The intense interest in K-12 reform will eventually exhaust all of the other options. The alternatives to competition are inevitable disappointments—that has already been proven many times.

Notes

1. The familiarity of the term *public school* trumps the more accurate *government-run school*. Not nearly enough people see and think about the government's schools as the government agencies they are. Nor do enough realize that attendance zones make the vast majority of public schools among the least public of government-provided services.

2. On exit versus voice, see Hirschman 1970.

3. My wife (then a teacher) received a copy of this story in her school mailbox from her principal, and it appeared again in a July 10, 2001, Education Intelligence Agency communiqué.

4. A former teacher told me that her district micromanaged teachers because parents compared them and asked why some teachers did more or used more effective methods than other teachers.

5. Attempts to ignore differences in students are sometimes labeled "mainstreaming" or following the common school ideal. Charter schools are a welcome, if minor, break from this pattern.

6. It would be very difficult to make student bodies more homogenous than public schools are now. A *Newsweek* cover story (J. Klein 1994) made that case, largely through the example of a particular and supposedly typical example. It included this statement: "Recent studies show that most school systems remain as profoundly segregated as those in Summerton, and those in the inner cities seem far more desperate." (27) According to Robert L. Carter, an NAACP lawyer who helped argue *Brown v. Board of Education,* "More black children are in all or virtually all black schools today than in 1954" ("Civil Rights Leaders" 1994).

7. School districts satisfy the definition of a *cartel:* an association of producers that curtails or significantly reduces competition. A school district is a much more stable anticompetitive institution than any cartel of

private firms or even a cartel of nations, such as the OPEC oil cartel. See, for example, Dougherty and Becker 1995.

8. Because of its consistency with other indicators of educational achievement (remedial education spending by colleges and businesses, other standardized tests), the inference derived from this terrible result survives the criticism that scores are low because students have no incentive to try hard. See Murphy 1996 (139–48) for more examples illustrating that student achievement is utterly unacceptable nearly everywhere.

9. The evidence is direct and indirect. The appalling test scores, including the embarrassing international comparisons, are based on the entire student population. Growing expenditures on remediation by businesses and colleges are not limited to inner-city high school graduates. Direct evidence of troubled suburban schools is offered in Singal 1991, and see "Dollars Don't Mean Success" (1997) on the troubles of a California school district that spends $12,100 per student per year. In San Antonio, Texas, community college–bound high school graduates must take the Texas Academic Skills Program (TASP) test to determine whether they can begin college courses without remediation. Thirty students from San Antonio's wealthiest district, the suburban Alamo Heights District, took the TASP test in September 1992. Of those 30 students, 22, 15, and 16 required math, English, and reading remedial courses, respectively. See also Greene, Peterson, and Du 1997 for a description of Milwaukee's dismal secular private schools; Farwell 1998 is about several California school districts; Clowes (2000a) discusses exploding remedial education spending by businesses, community colleges, and universities.

10. Per-pupil spending of private schools per year—approximately $3,116 (1993–94 data) according to the National Center for Education Statistics—was much lower than public schools' per-pupil expenditures of approximately $6,500. Both public and private schools underestimate their costs, but the underestimates are much larger for public schools (see Lieberman and Haar, in press). The fact that private schools managed to perform better than public schools at about half the cost is a stunning indictment of public schools. If the efficient sector of the education industry were not limited and starved for funds, much more would be possible.

11. The most recent example I've seen is given in Searcy 2001.

12. A similar proposal was rejected by the 1999 Texas legislature.

13. Snell (2001) points out that the use of vouchers serves as a "legal sanction" against public schools rather than as a vehicle to facilitate parental choice.

14. For vouchers as a general tool of government policy, that principle is well established. See Steurle 1998, 15.

15. The findings are based on data from Phoenix, Indianapolis, Atlanta, San Antonio, and Milwaukee. In each city, there are long waiting lists for half-tuition grants available only to low-income families. The latest privately funded partial low-income voucher program attracted 1.25 million requests for forty thousand vouchers.

16. The privately funded Edgewood Program is a possible exception. Nearly everyone is eligible for a voucher that fully covers the tuition of most existing private schools. It's too soon to tell whether the program's limitations will keep it from significantly changing the school choice menu in San Antonio, Texas.

17. Even for a choice program that fosters competition, I would still prefer to avoid the term *experiment*. Words have meaning, and *experiment* implies "untried," risk, and caution. More than two hundred years have passed since the publication of Adam Smith's *Wealth of Nations,* and it is no longer necessary or fruitful to think of competition as an experiment. See Coulson 1999 on the history of competition, markets, and choice in education.

18. California's Proposition 38 was the best hope for a real demonstration project.

19. The *Wall Street Journal* captioned a recent editorial (Epstein 2001) with a phrase that applies equally to studies of voucher users test scores: "Why conduct studies to confirm the obvious? The proposition that parents can tell which school is best for their child is another clear winner in the category of Heavy-Handed Announcement of the Hopelessly Obvious".

20. Another reason to be wary of assuming that the private sector won't change is that to teachers, a significant political group on this question, a rise in the market share of a private sector such as the one we have now means lower salaries. Private-school salaries are approximately two-thirds of public-school salaries (see Ballou and Podgursky 1997), although private-school teachers typically report higher levels of job satisfaction than

public-school teachers. Serious parental choice programs, however, can and should produce a private sector much different than the one we have now. In particular, salaries are likely to rise in a private sector not starved for cash and forced to compete against a free rival.

21. Current private-school capacity in Milwaukee is so small that the voucher program created little or no competitive pressure within the private sector. Until private-sector capacity catches up to the program expansion, every decent private school willing to accept the voucher sum as full payment will fill up.

22. Retrieved from CEO America Web site (ceoamerica.org), August 8, 2000.

23. The Texas Education Agency reported that the Edgewood District had 14,142 students in 1997–98 school year, with 90.3 percent of them qualifying as "economically disadvantaged."

24. Private schools located inside the Edgewood District receive $3,600 for a K–8 student and $4,000 for a grade 9–12 child. At the time the program went into effect, there were only four private schools in the district. Private schools located outside the Edgewood District receive $2,000 for a K–8 student and $3,500 for a grade 9–12 child.

25. Indiana just enacted charter legislation, so thirty-seven states have some sort of charter legislation on the books (Rees 2000).

26. Unlike a tax deduction, a tax credit reduces taxes by one dollar for every dollar spent on the credit good. A nonrefundable tax credit is limited to the amount of taxes paid; that is, if you spend more on the credit good than taxes paid, you do not get a refund. A nonrefundable tax credit is thus not available to the many poor people who pay no income tax.

27. Both Coulson (2001) and the Mackinac Center (with a similar proposal at http://www.SchoolChoiceWorks.org/) use the term *scholarship* in place of *voucher,* the term I prefer. Scholarship should mean that there are academic requirements for eligibility, but there are none. For that reason, it will mislead some potential applicants into not applying.

28. Arizona enrollment figures are estimated figures for 1999 from the National Center for Education Statistics.

29. For example, I would limit home schoolers' credit to actual education expenses.

30. Assuming a very restricted version of school choice, Levin and Driver estimate cost increases of up to 25 percent or more.

31. Some of the recent proposals are arguably exceptions; for example, some of Gary Johnson's voucher proposals and California's Proposition 38 would have been more than limited escape valves.

32. Lower-income families pay less than the cost of educating their children, whereas affluent families pay more than the cost of educating their children.

33. A similar article and headline appeared in the August 5, 1998, issue of *Education Week*.

34. Economics textbooks typically cite "many buyers and many sellers" as a feature of competitive industries.

35. This insightful phrase surfaces frequently. Milton Friedman (1998) said he heard it in a 1972 debate on Social Security from Wilbur Cohen, secretary of health, education, and welfare during the Johnson administration.

36. It is too soon to say whether San Antonio's Edgewood program contains enough of the key elements.

37. Even Milton Friedman (1998) refers to the Milwaukee and Cleveland programs as experiments.

38. For a detailed discussion of the inconsistency between Chubb and Moe's findings and policy recommendations, see West 1992.

39. She recently accepted a position on Vice President Cheney's staff.

40. More recently, Jack Klegg found that fewer than one thousand of the nation's twenty-six thousand private schools are nonsectarian, for-profit schools (1998, 20).

41. Seen most recently in the September 26, 2001, editorial "Cleveland Rocks" by the *Wall Street Journal* editorial board.

42. See Vedder 2000 for examples of such opportunities and how they can reduce teacher resistance to K–12 overhaul.

43. Much evidence indicates that zero government involvement is best. See, for example, Blumenfeld 1981 and Coulson 1999.

44. Much smaller tax changes have produced significant effects (see Whittington, Alm, and Peters 1990).

45. See D. B. Klein 1998 for more on certification and accreditation services in market economies.

46. Describing a typical urban school principal, Rexford Brown notes that "his greatest frustration is his inability to hire and fire his own teachers. You're the boss, but you're not able to hire and fire your own employees" (1993, 104).

47. Libertarians should note that Friedman-type proposals are the best and probably the only politically feasible way to achieve complete separation of school and state.

References

Aoki, Masato, and Susan F. Feiner. 1996. The Economics of Market Choice and At-Risk Students. In *Assessing Educational Practices*, edited by William E. Becker and William J. Baumol. Cambridge, Mass.: MIT Press.

Armor, David. 1997. *Competition in Education: A Case Study of Interdistrict Choice*. Boston: Pioneer Institute for Public Policy.

Ball, G. Carl. 1990. In Search of Educational Excellence. *Policy Review* (fall 1990): 54–55.

Ballou, Dale, and Michael Podgursky. 1997. *Teacher Pay and Teacher Quality*. Kalamazoo, Mich.: W.E. Upjohn Institute for Employment and Training.

Barro, Robert J. 1997. Can Public Schools Take Competition? *Wall Street Journal*, March 10.

Bast, Joseph L., and David Harmer. 1997. *Vouchers and Educational Freedom: A Debate*. Policy Analysis Monograph no. 269. Washington, D.C.: Cato Institute.

Baumol, William J., John C. Panzar, and Robert D. Willig. 1982. *Contestable Markets and the Theory of Industry Structure*. New York: Harcourt Brace Jovanovich.

Becker, William E., and William J. Baumol, eds. 1996. *Assessing Educational Practices*. Cambridge, Mass.: MIT Press.

Blumenfeld, Samuel. 1981. *Is Public Education Necessary?* Boise, Idaho: Paradigm.

Bonsteel, Alan, and Carlos A. Bonilla. 1997. *A Choice for Our Children*. San Francisco: ICS.

Borenstein, Severin. 1992. The Evolution of U.S. Airline Competition. *Journal of Economic Perspectives* 6 (spring): 45–74.

Bowman, Darcia H. 2000. States Giving Choice Bills Closer Look. *Education Week* (March 1): 1, 24.

Brandly, Mark. 1997. Home Schooling Leaps into the Spotlight. *Wall Street Journal,* June 9 XX.

Broder, David. 1999. Reforming Education: A Tough Assignment. *San Antonio Express-News,* March 2, 7B.

Brown, Rexford G. 1993. *Schools of Thought.* San Francisco: Jossey-Bass.

Carnegie Foundation for the Advancement of Teaching. 1992. *School Choice: A Special Report,* Princeton, N.J.: Carnegie Foundation.

Center for the Study of Public Policy. 1970. *Financing Education by Grants to Parents.* Washington, D.C.: U.S. Office of Economic Opportunity.

Choice Debate Is Over (editorial). 2000. *Wall Street Journal,* April 6.

Chubb, John, and Terry Moe. 1990a. *Educational Choice.* San Antonio: Texas Public Policy Foundation.

———. 1990b. *Politics, Markets, and America's Schools.* Washington, D.C.: Brookings Institution.

———. 1991. The Private vs. Public School Debate. *Wall Street Journal,* July 26.

Church and State. 1992: Voucher Advocate Says "Milwaukee Plan" Should be Exported (editorial). *Church and State,* May, 16–17.

Civil Rights Leaders Wear Scars of Controversy. 1994. *Washington Times,* May 17 XX.

Cleveland Rocks (editorial). 2001. *Wall Street Journal,* September 26.

Clowes, George A. 1998. Five Steps to Full School Choice. *School Reform News* (September): 10–11.

———. 2000a. The Dark Side of Suburban School Achievement. *School Reform News* (January): 7.

———. 2000b. Vouchers Lift Black Student Scores. *School Reform News* (November): 1, 6.

Coats, Dan. 1997. The Bell Is Sounding for School Choice: D.C. Example Shows Why Support for It Is Growing Inside Congress. *Roll Call,* June 2, 10.

Cohen, David K., and Eleanor Farrar. 1977. Power to the Parents. *The Public Interest* 48: 72–97.

Cookson, Peter. 1996. In *School Choice: Examining the Evidence,* edited by Edith Rasell and Richard Rothstein. Washington, D.C.: Economic Policy Institute.

Coons, John E., and Stephen D. Sugarman. 1978. *Education by Choice*. Berkeley: University of California Press.

Cordell, Dorman E. 1998. Answering Objections to School Vouchers in D.C. *National Center for Policy Analysis Brief Analysis* 266 (May 22): 1–2.

Coulson, Andrew. 1999. *Market Education*. New Brunswick, N.J.: Transaction.

———. 2001. *Toward Market Education: Are Vouchers or Tax Credits the Better Path?* Cato Policy Analysis Paper no. 392. Washington, D.C.: Cato Institute.

Danitz, Tiffany. 1997. Private Vouchers Are Going Public. *Insight* (September 8): 15.

Davis, Bob. 1996. Dueling Professors Have Milwaukee Dazed over School Vouchers. *Wall Street Journal*, October 11, A1.

Dixon, A. P. 1992. Parents: Full Partners in the Decision Making Process. *NASSP Bulletin* (April): 15–18.

Dollars Don't Mean Success in California District. 1997. *Education Week* (December 3).

Dougherty, J. Chrys, and Stephen L. Becker. 1995. *An Analysis of Public-Private School Choice in Texas*. San Antonio: Texas Public Policy Foundation.

Drury, Darrel W. 2000. Vouchers and Student Achievement. *Policy Research* (summer).

Economic Policy Institute. 1993. *School Choice: Examining the Evidence* Washington: EPI.

Education Policy Institute. 1999. New Poll Finds Public in Dark About Charters and Vouchers. *EPI-Update*, November 19.

Elmore, Richard, Gary Orfield, and Bruce Fuller. 1995. *School Choice: The Cultural Logic of Families, the Political Rationality of Institutions*. New York: Teachers College.

Epple, Dennis, and Richard E. Romano. 1998. Competition Between Private and Public Schools, Vouchers, and Peer Group Effects. *American Economic Review* 88 (March): 33–62.

Epstein, Joseph. 2001. "B is for Boys—and Bullies." *Wall Street Journal*, April 30.

Evans, W. N., and R. M. Schwab. 1995. Finishing High School and Starting College: Do Catholic Schools Make a Difference? *Quarterly Journal of Economics* CX (4):941-74.

Explosion in Home Schooling. 1996. *U.S. News and World Report* (February 12): 57–58.

Farwell, Kamrhan. 1998. Money Doesn't Always Equal High Test Scores. *The Press Enterprise,* August 10.

Finn, Chester E., Jr. 1995. The Schools. In *What to Do About . . .* , edited by N. Kozodny. New York: HarperCollins.

Finn, Chester E., and Rebecca L. Gau. 1998. New Ways of Education. *The Public Interest* (winter): 79.

Finn, Chester E., Bruno V. Manno, Louann A. Bierlein, and Gregg Vanourek. 1997. *Charter Schools in America Project: Final Report, Part 2.* Indianapolis, Ind.: Hudson Institute.

Fiske, Edward B., and Helen F. Ladd. 2000. *When Schools Compete: A Cautionary Tale.* Washington, D.C.: Brookings Institution Press.

Fondy, Albert. 1998. *School Vouchers in Pennsylvania: Bad Education Policy, Worse Public Policy.* Philadelphia: Pennsylvania Federation of Teachers.

Fox, Michael. 1997. Remarks of Ohio State Representative Michael Fox. In *State Legislator Guide to Teacher Empowerment.* Washington: American Legislative Exchange Council, 1997: p.17.

Friedman, Milton. 1955. The Role of Government in Education. In *Economics and the Public Interest,* edited by R. A. Solo. New Brunswick, N.J.: Rutgers University Press.

———. 1962. *Capitalism and Freedom.* Chicago: University of Chicago Press.

———. 1998. Freedom and School Vouchers. *Chronicles* (December).

Fuller, Howard. 1997. A Research Update on School Choice. *Marquette University Current Education Issues* 97, no. 3 (October): 1.

Goenner, James N. 1996. Charter Schools: The Revitalization of Public Education. *Phi Delta Kappan* 78, no. 1 (September): 32–34.

Goldhaber, Dan D. 1996. Public and Private High Schools: Is School Choice an Answer to the Productivity Problem? *Economics of Education Review* 15, no. 2: 93–109.

Goldwater Institute. 1994. *The Top Ten Myths about School Choice.* Phoenix, Ariz.: Goldwater Institute.

Greene, Jay P. 2000. Why School Choice Can Promote Integration. *Education Week* (April 12): 52.

Greene, Jay P., Paul Peterson, and Jiangtao Du. 1997. *The Effectiveness of School Choice: The Milwaukee Experiment.* Cambridge, MA: Program in Education Policy and Governance, Harvard University.

Hess, Frederick M. 1998. Courting Backlash: The Risks of Emphasizing Input Equity over School Performance. *Virginia Journal of Social Policy and the Law* 6 (fall): 13.

Hess, Frederick, Robert Maranto, and Scott Milliman. 1999. Coping with Competition: How School Systems Respond to School Choice. Working Paper.

Hicks, J. 1935. Annual Survey of Economic Theory: The Theory of Monopoly. *Econometrica* 3 (January).

Hirschman, Albert O. 1970. *Exit, Voice, and Loyalty.* Cambridge, Mass.: Harvard University Press.

Holland, Robert. 2000. Real Math: Sexist, Racist, or Just Hard. *School Reform News* (March): 1, 10.

Hoxby, Caroline. 2001. School Choice and School Productivity. Paper presented at the Conference on the Economics of School Choice, Islamorada, Florida. National Bureau of Economic Research, February 22–24.

Hume, Jerry. 1990. In Search of Educational Excellence. *Policy Review* (fall): 55.

Jencks, Christopher. 1966. Is the Public School Obsolete? *The Public Interest* 2: 18–27.

Jennings, Wayne B. 1998. Let's Ride the Wave of Change. *Enterprising Educators* 6, no. 2 (spring): 1.

Kantrowitz, Barbara, and Wingert, Pat. 1991. A Dismal Report Card. *Newsweek,* June 17, 1991: 65.

Kirkpatrick, David. 1997. *School Choice: The Idea That Will Not Die.* Mesa, Ariz.: Bluebird.

———. 1999. School Choice Choir Has a Broad Range of Voices. *School Reform News* (July): 9.

Klegg, Jack. 1998. Interview. *School Reform News* (October): 20.

Klein, Daniel B. 1998. Quality-and-Safety Assurance: How Voluntary Social Processes Remedy Their Own Shortcomings. *Independent Review* 2, no. 4: 537–55.

Klein, Joe. 1994. The Legacy of Summerton. *Newsweek* (May 16): 26–31.

Kronholz, June. 2000. In Michigan, Amway Chief and Wife Give School Vouchers a Higher Profile. *Wall Street Journal,* October 25.

Lamdin, Douglas J., and Michael Mintrom. 1997. School Choice in Theory and Practice: Taking Stock and Looking Ahead. *Education Economics* 5, no. 3: 235.

Levin, Henry M. 1968. The Failure of the Public Schools and the Free Market Remedy. *Urban Review* 2: 32–37.

———. 1992. Market Approaches to Education: Vouchers and School Choice. *Economics of Education Review* 11, no. 4: 279–85.

Levin, Henry M., and Cyrus E. Driver. 1997. Costs of an Education Voucher System. *Education Economics* 5, no. 3 (December): 265–83.

Lieberman, Myron. 1993. *Public Education: An Autopsy.* Cambridge, Mass.: Harvard University Press.

Lieberman, Myron, and Charlene Haar. In press. *The Real Cost of Public Education.* (New Brunswick, NJ: Transaction Press, 2002).

Lowe, Rob, and Barbara Miner. 1996. *Selling Out Our Schools.* Milwaukee, Wisc.: Rethinking Schools.

Maranto, Robert, and Scott Milliman. 1999. In Arizona, Charter Schools Work. *Washington Post,* October 11, A25.

McGroarty, Daniel. 1996. *Break These Chains.* Rocklin, Calif.: ICS, Prima.

———. 1998. *Voucher Wars: Strategy and Tactics as School Choice Advocates Battle the Labor Leviathan.* Issues in School Choice no. 2. Indianapolis, Ind.: Milton and Rose Friedman Foundation.

Meier, Deborah W. 1991. The Little Schools That Could. *The Nation* (September 23): 1, 338.

Merrifield, John. 1992. *School Choice: A Special Report.* Princeton, N.J.: Carnegie Foundation for the Advancement of Teaching.

———. 1993. *School Choice: Examining the Evidence.* Washington, D.C.: Economic Policy Institute.

Miller, D. W. 1999. The Black Hole of Education Research. *Chronicle of Higher Education* (August 6).

Moe, Terry. 2001. *Schools, Vouchers, and the American Public.* Washington, D.C.: Brookings Institution.

Morrison, Steven A., and Clifford Winston. 1987. Empirical Implications and Tests of the Contestability Hypothesis. *Journal of Law and Economics* 30 (April 1987): 53–66.

Murphy, Joseph. 1996. *The Privatization of Schooling*. Thousand Oaks, Calif.: Corwin.

Nathan, Joe, ed. 1989. *Public Schools by Choice*. St. Paul, Minn: Institute for Learning and Teaching.

National Commission on Excellence in Education. 1983. *A Nation at Risk: The Imperative for Educational Reform*. Washington, D.C.: U.S. Department of Education.

Nechyba, Thomas J. 2001. Introducing School Choice into Multi-District Public School Systems. Paper presented at the Conference on the Economics of School Choice, Islamorada, Florida. National Bureau of Economic Research, February 22–24.

Organization for Economic Cooperation and Development (OECD). 1995. *Education at a Glance: OECD Indicators*. Paris: OECD.

Pearson, Hugh. 1996. An Urban Push for Self-Reliance. *Wall Street Journal*, February 7.

Peterkin, Robert. 1996. Choice and Public School Reform. In *Selling Out Our Schools*, edited by Robert Lowe and Barbara Miner. Milwaukee, Wisc.: Rethinking Schools.

Peters, Tom. 1990. In Search of Educational Excellence. *Policy Review* (fall): 57–58.

Peterson, Paul E. 1997. A Report Card on School Choice. *Commentary* (October): 29–33.

Pfaff, Leslie. 2000. "The Right to Choose," *The New Jersey Monthly* (September 15, 2000).

Pierce, R. K. 1993. *What Are We Trying to Teach Them Anyway?* San Francisco: Institute for Contemporary Studies.

Price, Hugh B. 1999. Establish an Academic Bill of Rights. *Education Week* (March 17): 76, 54-55.

Quade, Quentin. 1996. *Financing Education*. New Brunswick, N.J.: Transaction.

———. 2000. Must Tax Dollars Kill School Independence? Blum Center Web site. Available at: www.marquette.edu/blum/taxkill.html. Accessed August 8.

Rand Corporation. 1977. *A Study of Alternatives in American Education* IV, VII. Santa Monica, Calif.: Rand Corporation.

Rasell, Edith, and Richard Rothstein. 1996. *School Choice: Examining the Evidence*. Washington, D.C.: Economic Policy Institute.

Ravitch, Diane. 2000. *Left Back*. New York: Simon and Schuster.

Rees, Nina S. 1999a. Johnson's Voucher Vision. *School Reform News* (November): 5.

———. 1999b. Public School Benefits of Private School Vouchers. *Policy Review* (January–February): 16–19.

———. 2000. *School Choice: What's Happening in the States*. Washington, D.C.: Heritage Foundation.

Richman, Sheldon. 2001. Sell the Schools. *Future of Freedom Foundation Editorial* (April).

Rickover, Hyman G. 1959. *Education and Freedom*. New York: E. P. Dutton.

Salganik, Laura H. 1981. The Fall and Rise of Education Vouchers. *Teachers College Record* 83, no. 2 (winter): 263–83.

Salisbury, David. 1997. Free to Choose: A Legislative Briefing on Education Reform and School Choice. *Sutherland Speeches* 8 (November): 1–17.

Sandham, Jessica L. 1999. Florida OKs 1st Statewide Voucher Plan. *Education Week* (May 5): 1, 21.

Sawhill, Isabel V., and Shannon L. Smith. 1998. Vouchers for Elementary and Secondary Education. In *Vouchers and Related Delivery Mechanisms: Consumer Choice in the Provision of Public Services*. Conference proceedings. Washington, D.C.: Brookings Institution.

Schnaiberg, Lynn. 1997. Firms Hoping to Turn Profit from Charters. *Education Week* (December 10): 14.

———. 1998. Charter Schools Struggle with Accountability. *Education Week* (June 10): 1, 14.

School Reform Blooms (editorial). 1999. *Wall Street Journal*, May 5.

School Reform News. 1998. Charters Killing Private Schools. *School Reform News* (November, 1998): 12.

———. 1999. Takeovers Don't Bring Turnaround in Student Achievement. *School Reform News* (May, 1999): 5.

School Vouchers on Trial in Milwaukee and Cleveland. 1998. *Mobilization for Equity* (February): 1, 3.

Searcy, Lesley. 2001. Changes Necessary to Give Students Equal Opportunity. *Birmingham News*, July 31.

Shokraii, Nina H. 1998. What People Are Saying about School Choice. *Heritage Foundation Backgrounder* 1188 (June 2): 1.

Singal, Daniel U. 1991. The Other Crisis in American Education. *Atlantic Monthly* (November): 59–74

Sizer, Ted, and Phillip Whitten. 1968. A Proposal for a Poor Children's Bill of Rights. *Psychology Today* 58: 59–63.

Smith, Kevin B., and Kenneth J. Meier. 1995. *The Case Against School Choice.* New York: M. E. Sharpe.

Snell, Lisa. 2001. *School Vouchers as a Legal Sanction.* Reason Public Policy Institute Policy Study no. 284. Los Angeles : Reason Public Policy Institute.

Solmon, Lewis C., Michael K. Block, and Mary Gifford. 2000. *A Market-Based Education System in the Making.* Phoenix, Ariz.: Goldwater Institute.

Steurle, Eugene. 1998. Common Issues for Voucher Programs. In *Vouchers and Related Delivery Mechanisms: Consumer Choice in the Provision of Public Services.* Washington, D.C.: Brookings Institution.

Sykes, Charles J. 1995. *Dumbing-Down Our Kids.* New York: St. Martin's.

Testa, William A., and Surya Sen. 1999. School Choice and Competition (conference summary). *Chicago Fed Letter* 143a (July).

Third International Mathematics and Science Study (TIMSS). *School Reform News,* April 1998: 1.

Tirozzi, Gerald. 1997. Vouchers: A Questionable Answer to an Unasked Question. *Education Week* (April 23): 64–65.

Toch, Thomas. 1998. The New Education Bazaar. *U.S. News and World Report* (April 27): 34–36.

Trujillo, Anthony. 1999. Interview in Wall-to-Wall, for All Children. *School Reform News* (February): 20, 16.

Texas State Teachers Association (TSTA) and National Education Association (NEA). 1994. *Our Public Schools: The Best Choice for Texas.* Austin: TSTA and NEA, mimeograph.

Two School Chiefs Talk about Vouchers (editorial). *School Reform News* (January): 10.

Vedder, Richard. 2000. *Can Teachers Own Their Own Schools?* Oakland, Calif.: The Independent Institute.

Viteritti, Joseph. 1999. *Choosing Equality: School Choice, the Constitution, and Civil Society.* Washington, D.C.: Brookings Institution.

Voliva, G. 1999. Public Support for Nonpublic Schools. Available at: *PrairieNet.org.* Accessed August 26.

Wagner, Tony. 1996. School Choice: To What End? *Phi Delta Kappan* 78, no. 1 (September): 71.

Walsh, Mark. 1998. Vouchers Face Key Legal Test in Wisconsin. *Education Week* (March 11).

———. 1999a. Giuliani Proposes a Voucher Program for New York. *Education Week,* (January 27): 3.

———. 1999b. Ground Zero for Vouchers. *Education Week* (March 17): 46–51.

West, Edwin G. 1967. Tom Paine's Voucher Scheme for Public Education. *Southern Economic Journal* 33: 378–82.

———. 1992. Autonomy in School Provision: Meanings and Implications (review essay). *Economics of Education Review* 11, no. 4: 417–25.

White, Kerry A.1999. Ahead of the Curve. *Education Week* (January 13): 34.

Whittington, Leslie A., James Alm, and H. Elizabeth Peters. 1990. Fertility and the Personal Exemption: Implicit Pronatalist Policy in the United States. *American Economic Review* 80, no. 3: 545–56.

Williams, Joe. 1998. MPS Guarantees Help for Poor Readers. *Milwaukee Journal Sentinel,* December 23.

Witte, John. 2000. *The Market Approach to Education.* Princeton, N.J.: Princeton University Press.

Witte, John F., Andrea B. Bailey, and Christopher A. Thorn. 1993. *Third Year Report, Milwaukee Parental Choice Program.* Madison: University of Wisconsin.

Witte, John F., and Mark E. Rigdon. 1993. Education Choice Reforms: Will They Change American Schools? *Publius: The Journal of Federalism* (summer): 95–114.

Index

JOHN D. MERRIFIELD is Professor of Economics at the University of Texas at San Antonio. He is the author of many academic articles in natural resource economics, regional economics and educational policy. Dr. Merrifield is the author of the recent book *The School Choice Wars* and is a frequent guest on television and radio on the issue of school choice.

INDEPENDENT STUDIES IN POLITICAL ECONOMY

For further information and a catalog of publications, please contact:
THE INDEPENDENT INSTITUTE
100 Swan Way, Oakland, California 94621-1428, U.S.A.
510-632-1366 • Fax 510-568-6040 • info@independent.org • www.independent.org